4 VIEWS ON TALKING TO TEENAGERS ABOUT SEX
Pragmatic Help for Teaching Sexuality

Mark Oestreicher, General Editor
Contributors:
Jen Bradbury
Jake Kircher
Jonathan McKee
Joel Stepanek

THE
YOUTH CARTEL

4 VIEWS ON TALKING TO TEENAGERS ABOUT SEX

ISBN-13: 978-1-942145-43-1
ISBN-10: 1-942145-43-8

The Youth Cartel, LLC
www.theyouthcartel.com
Email: info@theyouthcartel.com
Born in San Diego
Printed in the U.S.A.

CONTENTS

Introduction | *Mark Oestreicher*   5

View 1: Fostering Open, Positive Dialogue   11
Jake Kircher | Response by Joel Stepanek

View 2: Exposing Young People to Explicit Truth   37
Jonathan McKee | Response by Jen Bradbury

View 3: Developing a Sexual Ethic   69
Jen Bradbury | Response by Jonathan McKee

View 4: Embracing God's Design for Us and for Sex   99
Joel Stepanek | Response by Jake Kircher

Notes   124

Bios   128

INTRODUCTION

I've spent my 35+ years of youth ministry working with middle schoolers. As a result, how I've talked about sex with the teenagers in my churches has probably looked a little different than it does for those of you who work with high schoolers.

Two examples:

The overkill story: I once hosted a Parent/Teen Sex Retreat. I really should have named it something else, as that name was just so, so, so creepy. Sorry. But the name wasn't the worst part.

We had some fun and did retreat-y things, but the bulk of our time was spent in teaching and dialogue. I stood up front as a host, introducing topics and giving a bit of biblical framing. Young teens and their parent or parents sat in pairs and trios clustered around the room, with most of their time spent in dialogue. That sounds great, right? *Except*, I think I just made it way too awkward. I wanted them to talk about real stuff, rather than merely having a five-minute talk that followed this predictable outline:

> Parent: "So, I think we need to talk about sex."
> Teenager: (shudders, looks for escape route)
> Parent: "So…uh…we're wondering if you have any questions? You can ask us anything."
> Teenager: "Nope. No questions."
> Parent: "Awesome. I'm really glad we had this talk!"

I mean, the conversations I hosted on that retreat were pretty uncomfortable. I had parents share about their first sexual experience, and stuff like that. They were compliant enough. (I can't believe none of them walked out, or told me, "This is just too much!") All I know is that I'm glad I didn't take my own teenage children on a retreat like that with my church's youth ministry.

The silly story: Knowing that talking about sex with middle schoolers instantly leads to panic or snickering or both, I wanted a way to both "normalize" the topic and remove the tension. So I developed *The Sex Song*. Any time we were going to talk about sex (which we did at least once a year for a couple weeks), we started by singing this song. I can't share the tune here in this book, but the lyrics were:

> *Sex, sex, God gave us sex*
> *Sex, sex, God gave us sex*
> *And he made it for two specific purposes*
> *MAKING BABIES!* (shouted)
> *and*
> *SHOWING LOVE AND AFFECTION TO YOUR SPOUSE!*
> (likewise shouted)
> *Sex, sex, God gave us sex*

Honestly, the song was a winner. After the first few seconds (which were filled with facial expressions approximating either "What the heck?" or "Are we allowed to sing this in church?"), my middle schoolers totally got into it. It worked perfectly to disarm and normalize, and we were able to move into whatever specific topic was planned without as much weirdness.

Except, they loved the song so much they wanted to sing it all the time, even when we weren't teaching a sex series. They sang it at the top of their lungs in a McDonald's, once, on a mission trip. They sang it in the hallways of the church. It certainly made me wonder if I'd created a problem for myself!

Null curriculum
Curriculum developers (to be clear: curriculum means just "what you teach") talk about a wide variety of curriculums present in any intentional or unintentional teaching time. These include:

- *Formal curriculum* (what you intend to teach)

- *Hidden/covert curriculum* (all the variables of your learning environment that aren't openly communicated, but still transmit tons of "lessons," including norms, values, and beliefs)
- *Non-formal/experiential curriculum* (learning—hopefully intentionally—that happens when we're doing things together)
- *Null curriculum* (read on…)

This last one—null curriculum—is likely the one you've not heard of. It is, quite simply, the topics we do *not* talk about. Read this carefully, as it's important: **what we avoid talking about teaches just as much as what we choose to talk about.**

For example: if you don't ever talk about sex and sexuality with your teenagers, you're communicating a bunch of unhelpful, even inaccurate, lessons about sex and sexuality. You're teaching that God/the Bible/church don't have anything to say about this topic; you're teaching that Christianity is disconnected from the topics that are important to the teenage experience; you're probably even teaching a subtle "sex is dirty and shouldn't be talked about" negative message, which is completely out of alignment with God's desires and intent for creation.

I find that sex is part of the null curriculum in most homes (including Christian homes), and in the majority of youth groups. And that's a huge problem, particularly since our teenagers are indigenous to a hyper-sexualized culture where they're receiving massive quantities of harmful messages about sex on a daily basis.

In short: we *have* to talk about this!

Everything or nothing

A number of years ago I was helping an author develop a youth ministry resource on the topic of sex, and he said something that has stuck with me: *Most youth workers talk about sex as if it's everything, or as if it's nothing.* Both of these extremes are, really, dishonest.

Sex isn't everything. When I hear people say that teenagers are a "walking ball of hormones," I get uncomfortable. In one sense, this is close to accurate, developmentally. Yes, teenagers are being enormously impacted by the (God-given!) hormones that are bringing unprecedented changes to their bodies, minds, emotions, relationships, and faith. But when people make proclamations like that, they are usually implying that teenagers think about nothing but sex, 24/7/365. And it just ain't true. There's at least a bit of video games or nail polish color in there.

Yes, sex and sexuality (those two are not exactly the same thing) are huge issues for teens, as, I would suggest, God intended them to be. But they aren't everything. To say or imply that they are would be misleading.

But sex sure isn't nothing (apologies for the double-negative). While we shouldn't obsess over it, we should be committed to making it one of our top five or ten topics we talk about with teenagers.

Why 4 views?

We developed this line of *Views* books to provide youth workers with practical dialogue on topics that can sometimes be polarizing. The first book in this line—*4 Views on Pastoring LGBTQ Teenagers*— allowed us to prove that we can have civil, respectful dialogue, focused more on practice than theology. Not that we think theological discussion, even debate, isn't important. It certainly is. And it will be overtly clear that each of the four contributors in this book is theologically grounded, and is writing from biblical/ theological anchors (which is why we had them each include their theological anchors in an early section within their chapters).

But the point of this book is to offer you pragmatic help. And these four diverse youth workers are here to offer that to you.

How we talk about sex with teenagers deserves thought, prayer, and reflection. And *what* we talk about (and what outcomes we're hoping for) clearly needs to go deeper than "don't do it."

For this book's contributors, we were very careful—and took our time—to choose four articulate youth workers, who:

- had years of experience with talking to real teenagers about sex. We wanted writers who were "in the trenches," but had worked out their thinking through some years of trial and error.
- were diverse from one another in their perspectives and desired outcomes.

We also asked each of them to write a response to one of the other views. The intent of this is to provide a bit of clarity on differing points of view, and to offer some pushback to each other's takes on the topic.

I've gone back and forth about whether or not I should give you a heads up or summary of each of the views. Ultimately, I want you (the reader) to discover these, rather than be predisposed, or even make a pre-conclusion, about if you will be open to learning from each contributor. But I'll give you this: one word that I believe captures the primary focus or highest value for each author (which, really, you'll see reflected in the chapter titles we collaboratively came up with for them).

- Jake: *Honesty*
- Jonathan: *Truth*
- Jen: *Ownership*
- Joel: *Design*

That's a little tease for you, to whet your appetite.

Oh, and it's a coincidence that the four writers are all J names: Jake, Jonathan, Jen, and Joel. I regularly called them "the 4 Js" when communicating with them. Maybe they should form a band or something.

We hope reading this dialogue will have an impact on more than just your thinking, though that's a great place to start. Our greater hope is that these ideas will show up in your practice, and that teenagers will be helped in this wonderful and amazing and terrifying and potentially damaging area of their lives. Let's get sex out of our null curriculum.

And feel free to use my sex song.

– Mark Oestreicher
The Youth Cartel

VIEW 1: FOSTERING OPEN, POSITIVE DIALOGUE

BY JAKE KIRCHER

"What are they doing?" the seventh-grade guy, puzzled, asked me at the Smithsonian's National Zoo on a mission trip in Washington, DC. A group of us had gone with an elementary school summer program on a field trip and while we were at the exhibit with the deer, two decided to get a little frisky. The inner city second and third graders were pointing and laughing, yet here was this seventh grader in our group who honestly had no idea what was happening.

Dumbfounded, I tried to gently point him in the right direction by telling him the deer were making a baby. I was pretty shocked when all that led to was a more confused look on his face. It dawned on me that this kid had never had the talk from his very conservative mom or his completely out-of-the-picture dad. For whatever reason, I went the exact opposite direction to clarify what was happening. "That one is putting its penis into that one's vagina," I bluntly told him. As that sank in, I watched his jaw slowly drop and tears come into his eyes. He turned and walked away from the group to process the information I had just given him.

That was the first time I had given "the talk" to a teenager and I was honestly afraid I had broken him. I immediately began to worry about what kind of phone call I was going to get from his mom after the trip. Thankfully, by the grace of God, the phone call with his mom when we got back was very positive. She was embarrassed that she had never had that conversation with her son and asked me to take him out for ice cream to do it for her, man-to-man. I realized that I was going to need a much better plan for that discussion than what I did on the fly at the zoo.

As I prepared for that conversation, I spent a lot of time reflecting on the talks about sex that I had received when I was growing up. Unintentionally, my first lesson about sex was largely negative. The whole reason that I got "the talk" in the first place was because three of our senior pastor's daughters had gotten pregnant out of wedlock over a two-year span, and one had just announced she was pregnant for a second time. My innocent first response to this—"If God wanted her to have a baby, why is that a bad thing?"—was replaced with the truth of where babies come from and why church leadership was so disappointed. In "the talk," I was given the typical messages of Christian purity culture: "don't," "stop," "repress," "bounce your eyes," "inappropriate," "sex is wrong outside of marriage," and "you shouldn't look at that." Overall, I came to believe that sex should be avoided or repressed, that it was dangerous and something to fear or be ashamed of.

This mindset left me with a sense of shame and embarrassment about sex not just in my teenage years, but it also had a significant negative impact on my sex life even within marriage. Think of it in terms of an experiment. You place a dog inside an empty room and throw a bone in with him. Every time the dog tries to get the bone, you give him an electric shock. You continue that for some time. What will the dog do when you finally offer him the bone without the shock? Yeah... It has taken me years, and plenty of counseling, to work through the consistent negative messaging that I internalized about sex in my youth.

There is nothing more fulfilling, joyful, and connection-building in a marriage than sex—but there is also nothing in a marriage that can bring more shame, embarrassment, and insecurity. How you will see and experience sex in adulthood is dictated in large part by what you are taught about sex growing up. As youth workers, it is imperative to our teenagers' future relationships and marriages that we, along with their parents, help them develop and own a positive, healthy, biblical view of sexuality.

MY ASSUMPTIONS AND THEOLOGICAL ANCHORS

Sex is very good

Throughout my adult years I have had to unlearn much of the negative messaging I received about sex growing up. The starting point for a healthier, biblical view of sex was the fact that it is very good. Although the more poetic version of creation in Genesis 1 and the more narrative account of creation in Genesis 2 contrast one another in certain ways, one thing they are consistent about is that sex is a God-given blessing:

"God blessed them and said to them, 'Be fruitful and increase in number; fill the earth and subdue it…' God saw all that [was] made, and it [including sex] was very good." Genesis 1:28, 31 (emphasis and bracketed words added)

That is why a man leaves his father and mother and is united to his wife, and they become one flesh. Adam and his wife *were both naked, and they felt no shame*." Genesis 2:24-25 (emphasis added)

Let's look at other examples of reproductive methods in God's creation. God could have wired humans in a myriad of ways.

- Nearly thirty percent of male praying mantises experience what's known as sexual cannibalism post-coitus: i.e., the female eats the male after sex.
- When a honeybee reaches climax while mating with the queen, his testicles explode and the male dies.

- In order to find out if a female giraffe is in heat, the male will rub her rear end with his head until she pees and then he will drink it to find out if she is ready to be impregnated.

Seriously, you can have fun for hours googling "weird animal reproduction facts." The bottom line is that God had a lot of options. God didn't have to design sex between humans to be so powerfully bonding and potentially mutually pleasurable, but God did.

The Bible's high view of sexual intimacy is repeatedly used to give us a glimpse of the relationship God wants to have with each one of us. In the Jewish Scriptures, the exact same Hebrew word (*yadá*, meaning "to know") is used to denote both humans' ability to *know* God as well as the way a couple *knows* one another in the act of sex. In the New Testament, the image of marriage, which by definition includes sex (more on this later), is repeatedly used to depict our union with the bridegroom Christ.

John Philip Newell writes about this dynamic in his book *The Rebirthing of God:*

> True sexual relationship is regarded as an experience of the Divine because in such engagement we forget our separateness. Our whole being moves as one with the other in an enfolding and intermingling that goes deeper than our differences. True union delights in difference. It does not smother it. This is as true of the universe's oneness as it is in our most intimate relationships of longing. It is the bliss that can inspire us as a whole people as much as it delights us as lovers in union.[1]

Sex, as designed by the God who created each of us, is amazing, awesome, giving, fulfilling, powerful, fun, pleasurable, a gift, a blessing, bonding, and very good.

If sex is all of those good things, and God also created us, males and females, in God's image (Genesis 1:27), logically that also means that our bodies, physical beauty, attraction, and the desire to engage in sexual activity are all very good. Let's think of this another way.

Can you imagine what sex would be like if God hadn't biologically wired us to be attracted to a mate? Or if God didn't design us with nerve endings all over our bodies that are stimulated throughout the process of sex? Or what if, emotionally and neurologically, we didn't have a desire for sex but solely engaged in an act of procreation when our mate was in heat? Sex would be functional, much like going to the bathroom or eating a meal.[2]

Sex isn't just intercourse, but so much more

This leads us to the next theological assumption that is important to understand: sex isn't just intercourse, but so much more. Hillary McBride, an author, podcast host, and clinical counselor, defines sexuality as "the physical, emotional, psychological, and spiritual energy that permeates, influences, and colors our entire being and personality in its quest for love, communion, friendship, wholeness, self-perpetuation, and self-transcendence."[3] Sex isn't limited to one singular act of inserting a penis into a vagina. Our sexuality is expressed in multiple acts of touching, kissing, embracing, teasing, flirting, language and sound, facial expressions, and more. It's all part of God's amazing biological design to take our bodies, emotions, and minds through a process of pleasure and connection with another person.

Let's look a bit more at the science behind sex. According to Dr. Joe S. McIlhaney, Jr. and Dr. Freda McKissic Bush in their book *Hooked*, sex is defined as "any intimate contact between two individuals that involves arousal, stimulation, and/or a response by at least one of the two partners."[4] They go on in the book to talk about how sex begins in the brain as it prepares our bodies physically for intercourse. From the simple starting point of staring into one another's eyes or having a long embrace all the way through cuddling after intercourse, the brain releases neurochemicals—vasopressin in men and oxytocin in women—that develop synapses that tell us that we can trust the person we are with. All of this creates a stronger emotional bond. These two doctors, who lead the Medical Institute for Sexual Health, concluded based on their neurological and medical research that humans are biologically and neurologically designed to have the healthiest and best expressions of sexuality within lifelong, committed relationships.

Biblically speaking, sex equals marriage

This leads to an assumption and theological anchor that I believe is most often missed in conversations about sexuality with teenagers: biblically speaking, sex is the defining act that signifies when two people became one and are considered married. Author and theologian Scot McKnight writes, "there is no such thing as 'premarital' intercourse in the Bible. Intercourse…constitutes the sexual union that we call marriage."[5] By this definition, there is no such thing as casual or recreational sex because simply put, in the Bible, sex establishes a marriage.

Understanding this truth has led me to conclude that one of the biggest idols in the Christian faith today is the institution of marriage. We need to understand that the system of and requirements for becoming married, as we in our Western culture most commonly think of them, are not of a biblical design, but instead come from a man-made, cultural design. Yes, the Bible, starting in Genesis 1, does talk about the *concept* of marriage and the idea of Adam and Eve being united as husband and wife. But notice what's missing: there is no wedding ceremony, no exchanging of vows, no marriage license from the town clerk, and no pronouncement from an officiant. Yet today, many of us would look at a cohabitating couple who is having sex as sinful and wrong. In other words, if they haven't done any of those things, they therefore aren't married.

We don't find any of the elements we've come to accept and expect to accompany marriage—the license, the ceremony, the vows, etc.—anywhere in Scripture. Nor is there teaching about the liturgy of a wedding ceremony or guidelines on how to officiate a wedding. That's because they didn't exist until at least the 1300s. As historian Stephanie Coontz explains,

> Until the twelfth century the Church held that a marriage was valid if entered into by mutual consent and then sealed by sexual intercourse. This made nonconsummation grounds for

annulment. Then, in the mid-twelfth century, Peter Lombard, Bishop of Paris, argued that if sex was necessary for a valid marriage, Mary and Joseph could not have been legally married. In Lombard's view, a promise to wed ("words of the future") did not create a marriage unless it was followed by sex, but he insisted that an exchange of consent in the present—"I take you as my husband" and "I take you as my wife"—made a marriage legally and sacramentally binding even if the couple did not engage in sex. Lombard's views became official church teaching.[6]

What's even more fascinating to consider is exactly *why* the Catholic Church at the time decided to adopt Bishop Lombard's views. As unpacked by Coontz, the reasons were twofold and derived from a desire for control and power. One, the Church wanted to standardize a way to document, through church records, who they understood as married so that they could better enforce the Church's prohibition against divorce. Two, they realized that having power over who was getting married allowed for more financial gain for the Church, as they were able to charge families for the service of performing a wedding.

It took some time for these views to result in the legal and religious requirements we lean on for marriages today. In fact, it wasn't until the 1700s that obtaining a marriage license from a government entity and having a licensed officiant perform the wedding were officially established as the law of the land and of the Church.[7] Even by a conservative estimate, for almost ninety-five percent of human existence, marriage has been culturally initiated by consent and consummated by sex. Yet it seems today, especially in faith circles, that when we think of establishing a marriage we place all the emphasis on the five percent that took on importance in recent history—the license, the ceremony, the vows.

Wedding services, the exchanging of vows, and an officiant's pronouncement are wonderful liturgical and ceremonial elements that remind us of the power and importance of becoming married. However, they only make a couple husband and wife in the eyes of a religious institution or culture. In fact, since it's impossible for a pastor or justice of the peace to present two people as one flesh, putting so much emphasis on their pronouncement, however well-intentioned, actually robs sex of its power. Similarly, a marriage license is a great thing as it gives a couple certain tax and legal opportunities, but the piece of paper only makes someone married in the eyes of the government. Biblically, it is when two people who have committed to a relationship join themselves together into one flesh through the power of sex that they become married in God's eyes.

We need to treat all sin equally

My last assumption has less to do with a theology of sex and more to do with our overall posture toward what we define as sinful sexual behaviors. It seems that of all sins, those related to sex have gotten the most attention within our Christian culture. I have always found it disheartening and sad that when a woman gets pregnant out of wedlock or when a man comes out of the closet as gay, they often will disappear from our churches because they feel judged and shamed. If they don't disappear, they often are quickly rejected from being in any kind of leadership role within many church communities. Somehow what is defined as sin in the area of the sexual expression disqualifies them from positions of influence, and they are treated at times like a virus that, if not contained immediately, will influence others in a negative way.

Yet, at the exact same time that we are addressing these "sinners" in our churches, the women's ministry is running rampant with gossip, business leaders who serve on our leadership teams are engaging in cutthroat behaviors to get to the top of the corporate world, and senior leaders are driven by pride and the need to control others. Beyond that, there are any number of people in our churches engaging in behaviors that many would define as sinful but that are never actually addressed, simply because most people know they're best left private. When it comes to sex, we often penalize the people who aren't smart or lucky enough to keep their sins hidden, or who decide to be vulnerable and take the risk of being honest about what they may be struggling with. Everyone else gets a free pass. Frankly, if we addressed all sinful behavior the way we treat public revelations of sexual sin, we'd have no one left in church leadership.

This tendency to condemn sexual sin overtly and aggressively is one important reason why many of those who grow up in the church hold a negative view of sexuality. Whether it's done intentionally or not, it makes sexual acts the unforgivable sins and leaves many people thinking that their desires, and especially any actions born out of those desires, are shameful and perverted. I remember feeling exactly this way in high school while I was a student leader in my youth group and also looking at porn and masturbating at home. There were so many times I wanted to talk to one of my youth leaders about it and ask for help, but I never did because I was terrified of, at best, getting kicked off leadership, or, at worst, being called a pervert and asked not to come to youth group anymore.

In the Sermon on the Mount, Jesus addresses the law and how he views it differently than the religious leaders of the day:

> "Do not think that I have come to abolish the Law or the Prophets; I have not come to abolish them but to fulfill them. For truly I tell you, until heaven and earth disappear, not the smallest letter, not the least stroke of a pen, will by any means disappear from the Law until everything is accomplished. Therefore anyone who sets aside one of the least of these commands and teaches others accordingly will be called least in the kingdom of heaven, but whoever practices and teaches these commands will be called great in the kingdom of heaven. For I tell you that unless your righteousness surpasses that of the Pharisees and the teachers of the law, you will certainly not enter the kingdom of heaven." (Matthew 5:17-20)

Understanding the fact that Jesus came to *fulfill* the law changes the entire way we should understand law and rules within religious expression. Also, the tongue in cheek nature of Jesus saying that only those whose "righteousness *surpasses* that of the Pharisees" emphasizes this even more. That line doesn't mean that we need to work harder. Instead, Jesus is making the point that *our* righteousness won't ever get it done, but Christ's righteousness, thanks to the cross, will. Paul addresses this same issue in Romans 8:3-4:

For what the law was powerless to do because it was weakened by the flesh, God did by sending his own Son in the likeness of sinful flesh to be a sin offering. And so [God] condemned sin in the flesh, in order that the righteous requirement of the law might be fully met in us, who do not live according to the flesh but according to the Spirit.

What this means for Christ followers today is that Christ's death made the law completely irrelevant. Following Christ does not mean following rules legalistically to prove our worth and earn God's love. Rather, what we see throughout the Sermon on the Mount is that every "you heard it said, but now I say to you…" statement is a twofold message. The first is a reminder to us that it's impossible to completely follow the law. Not committing adultery at first seems very achievable, but when Jesus adds that "anyone who looks at a woman lustfully has already committed adultery with her in his heart" (Matthew 5:28), no one can live up to the standard. This is the second part of the message of Jesus's teaching: living in the kingdom of God isn't just about following certain rules, it's about being the kinds of people who think more deeply about how we live and why we do the things we do.

People shouldn't be shamed away from our communities or disqualified from leadership just because they break a rule or "sin" (the apostle Paul would have been disqualified by these standards, as he admits in Romans 7:15 that "what I want to do I do not do, but what I hate I do"), but instead each of us should be looking at the kind of person we are trying to be. All of us need the same grace and love of God as we humbly and gently (see Galatians 6) challenge one another in how we live in *every* area of our lives, not just when it comes to sex.

MY PRIORITIES

Communicate a positive message about sex
As a teenager, I was told both by my parents and in church that sex

was a God-given, good thing. However it was very uncommon for an affirmation about sex not to be followed by any number of "but..." clarifying statements. I have vivid memories of a middle school sex education class at my Christian school where a speaker introduced the topic by telling us that sex was good (with the caveat of "when you're married"). Then the speaker had a medical doctor get up and spend the entire forty-five minute class explaining all the reasons why sex was dangerous and should be avoided.

We do need to help teens think about the undesired consequences of sex (I'll address this more in the next section). The problem is that when teens hear far more "buts" than anything else, the "buts" often bear the biggest influence on shaping their view of sex, distorting the theological truth that sex is very good. When communicating with teenagers about sex, my number one priority is to frame things from a positive standpoint as much as possible.

The teens we work with need to be told that God thinks sex is awesome and amazing. They need to understand the creativity that God has shown through the reproductive systems of all the species, and that we could have been wired for sex in any number of ways. They should be taught how bonding and emotionally impactful two people becoming one flesh can be. And they need to be told that the ability to create a human being with another person isn't a negative consequence, but an amazing gift from God.

Part of communicating a positive message about sex is telling our teens that their desire for sex is totally and completely normal. In my teenage years, every single time my sexual desires were caught by an adult, the adult responded with great disappointment and stern warnings. A healthy theology of sex places God as the creator and source of our sexual desires. So why would we react by showing anger or trying to instill a sense of shame when teenagers are simply living into the biology that God gave them, and all of us?

We should start talking about sex by affirming our youth's attraction to others' physical beauty. Attraction is the acknowledgement that another person looks good to us and that they have certain features that catch our eye and draw our attention. Attraction is what causes us to do a double take or mention how great another person looks. There is nothing wrong with this. In fact, it actually affirms the creativity and beauty that God displays in human creation. All kinds of people, with all kinds of shapes and attributes, can be attractive. As the saying goes, "Beauty is in the eye of the beholder." We must first behold in order to find the unique beauty in people.

We need to think about how to respond well when teens express actions and thoughts that go beyond expressing this basic attraction. When a parent catches their kid looking at pornography, when a teenager admits to one of their youth leaders that they are masturbating a lot, or even if it comes out that two of the youth you work with have hooked up, the first message they need to hear is that it is one hundred percent normal to be curious and to want to experience sexual intimacy and pleasure. The outward expressions of a desire for sex should almost mark a rite of passage, one where it is celebrated that our kids are growing up and heading toward adulthood.

Foster an open and welcome posture toward conversation and questions about sex

Once we've created a culture that affirms teens' desires for and interest in sex, my second priority is fostering an open and welcome posture toward conversation and questions. All teenagers should know that they can talk to their parents, pastors, and youth leaders about sex and ask any question they want.

I believe it's the lack of this open and welcome posture toward conversations about sex that drives some teenagers into an addiction with pornography. They have completely normal questions and curiosity, but often don't know who they can talk to about them. In worst-case situations, they have tried to ask an adult and in return had really uncomfortable conversations or received watered-down answers, which can easily result in them feeling lied to. So instead of having a healthy talk with a trusted adult, they turn to Google, which leads straight to answers that don't focus at all on relationships, and often aren't guided by any moral compass. From there, it's easy to access all sorts of dark places on the Internet.

Beyond simply letting them know they can ask any question, we also need to show teens that the responses to their questions will be completely honest and trustworthy. This means we should be willing to share both the good things and the more challenging aspects of sex. In my experience, lectures can be educational—but much more powerful and lastingly impactful are relationships, where dialogue goes back and forth, questions can be asked, and emotions can be expressed. These conversations are what carry the most weight for the teenagers we work with.

It's also within this context of honest conversation that we should be willing to dive into the practical realities and more humorous side of intimate moments. Most of our teenagers will have conjured images, and thus expectations, about sex that come from pornography or movies. We do them a disservice if we allow them to think that those carefully edited and choreographed scenes are the norm. We need to be open and forthright about the things that writers very often leave out when putting together their scripts:

- When you are undressing one another and the guy can't get the girl's bra undone or her sweater gets stuck on her head trying to take it off.

- When you reach the point where you need to stop to think about birth control.

- When you're going at it and another person pops into your thoughts—maybe even a family member.

- When you really want to have sex and your significant other just isn't in the mood and it's hard not to take it personally.

- When in the middle of having sex there is a noise that sounds like one of you just farted—where did that come from?

- When you're ready to have intercourse and the guy tries to put "it" in by repeatedly jabbing in the general area.

- When you're in the middle of a moment of passion and a child yells, "DAAAADDDYYY, I'M ALL DONE POOOOOPING!"
- When he finishes rather quickly and she is nowhere close to having an orgasm.
- When you're all done and you have to clean up before everything gets all over the place.

Sex is amazing and good, but it's also awkward and hilarious. Embracing some of that humor and talking about the less "sexy" realities of sex is a big part of developing a godly view of sexuality, one that will serve teens both now and later in life. If we want our teens to have healthy and realistic expectations about sex, the best way to do that is through open and honest conversation.

Help teens understand God's design for sexual expression
My third priority in communicating about sex to teenagers is helping them understand what God's desire is for their sexual expression. What I have bluntly told teenagers and parents for years as I have spoken on this subject is that "God's goal is *not* that you would be a virgin when you get married." Consciously or unconsciously, this goal has been communicated by many churches and faith organizations wanting to instill a culture of purity in teens. The problem, though, is that communicating that virginity is God's goal for us is completely divorced from the fact that sex equals marriage. And when we ignore that fact, we fall short of God's actual desire for our sexuality in a few ways.

First, it creates a "how close to the line can I get without going over?" mentality when it comes to sexual activity. In other words, the emphasis on virginity enforces the idea that God's goal for sexual purity is simply making sure we don't have intercourse before a marriage ceremony. Other sexual acts—oral sex, hand jobs, foreplay, etc.—get put into an interesting gray area and aren't looked at as real sex. (Interestingly, many Christians cite Bill Clinton's famous "I did not have sexual relations with that woman" line as instigating the loosening of the definition of what counts as sex and what doesn't. I think, though, that the church's own purity culture and emphasis on virginity have contributed much more to this changing definition.)

Second, emphasizing virginity has very often been associated with the idea that if you save sex for marriage, God will bless that by giving you really great sex with your spouse. Having attended a Christian college, I know many people, including my wife and me, who were able to save virginity until marriage. Yet most of these people, again including my wife and me, didn't encounter any special blessing in our sex lives because of that. In fact, we experienced just the opposite: normal discomfort, awkwardness, humor, and difficulty navigating around the bedroom physically and emotionally as two people trying to do something we had never done before.

Maintaining your virginity doesn't guarantee sexual compatibility once you're married. The normal process of practicing and learning sexual compatibility should be something our teens, through the kinds of open and honest conversations I mentioned earlier, have knowledge of long before they say "I do."

Third, communicating that God's goal for our sexuality is that we would maintain our virginity until marriage lays the groundwork for a dangerous, shame-based understanding of sex. Similar to the way a more liberal culture might use virginity to make fun of or pressure someone who hasn't had sex, our Christian version of appropriate sexual activity creates a "godly" hierarchy that makes teens who have had sex feel less than, both in the eyes of their church community and of God. This line of thinking limits the power of the cross and the gift of grace that Jesus gives to all of us freely and generously. Instead, it communicates the idea that salvation and sanctification are in our hands, things to be earned through our own efforts.

So, if God's will isn't for us to remain virgins until we are married, what is it? I believe God's desire for our sex life is best summarized in 1 Thessalonians 4:3-8:

> It is God's will that you should be sanctified: that you should avoid sexual immorality; that each of you should learn to control

your own body in a way that is holy and honorable, not in passionate lust like the pagans, who do not know God; and that in this matter no one should wrong or take advantage of a brother or sister. The Lord will punish all those who commit such sins, as we told you and warned you before. For God did not call us to be impure, but to live a holy life. Therefore, anyone who rejects this instruction does not reject a human being but God, the very God who gives you his Holy Spirit.

Putting this a different way, God's desire for how we express our sexuality is that we would be holy—sanctified, pure, perfect, sacred, revered, and divine (to name just a handful of synonyms). This is so much bigger and deeper than a black and white rule about not inserting a penis into a vagina. Being challenged to be holy in our sexuality and to "avoid sexual immorality" leads us away from the oversimplified question of "how close to the line can I get?" Instead, when we focus on holiness, we will find ourselves putting other people before ourselves and living in a way that honors and loves others as brothers and sisters in Christ. This requires a totally different mindset, one that's not rooted in legalism, but one that spends time in deep and purposeful thought about how we live out our sexuality.

Notice that the passage doesn't mention marriage, nor even come close to saying "don't have sex." Instead, it says that sex is holy, and because it is holy, the Thessalonians shouldn't express it any and every way they want to. If we refuse to "wrong" (the Greek word is *pleonekteō*, meaning "overreach or take advantage") or "take advantage" (the Greek here is *hyperbainō*, meaning "to overstep or go beyond") of another person, as that passage instructs, it's clear that we certainly shouldn't take it from another person whenever we want it. This passage illustrates that when it comes to sexual expression, we shouldn't think only about our own well-being and desires but must also consider the impact on the person we're thinking about or with physically.

Put sex in context

My last priority for this important, ongoing conversation with teenagers is that we have to do a better job of putting sex in context, and that means talking more, and being willing to teach more, about marriage. In my years as a youth pastor at a church, I always included a week dedicated to this topic in our annual series on sex, called *Everything You Need to Know if You Ever Want to Get Married*. It was always one of our most popular weeks.

The central point I always made in this series is that, biblically speaking, sex equals marriage. In many ways, this flips the typical purity culture mantra of "wait until marriage" on its head. Rather than telling teens to save sex for marriage, which results in a dualistic mindset about bad sex versus good sex, putting sex in context teaches the fact that God's design for sex is *so* powerful and good that, emotionally, neurologically, and spiritually, it is what makes two people become one flesh. This perspective leads to a question for teens about whether they are ready for the kind of commitment sex wires us to make. It *then* leans into some of the reasons why, if they aren't ready to be married, they should think twice about engaging in an act that, in God's eyes, makes you married.

The fact is, our teens are learning every day about marriage. They are watching their parents, their friends' parents, their youth leaders and pastors, movies, and TV shows. To argue that they don't want to talk about marriage or that they are too young to discuss marriage is being naïve. Not talking about it means we're limiting what they learn about marriage to their internal observations, reality TV, and once again, Google. We spend most of childhood preparing our kids for the future: college, career, faith, and more. Why shouldn't we also focus on marriage—the most important relationship they will ever have? Is it surprising divorce rates are as high as they are when we save the vast majority of teachings on marriage for a random amount of premarital counseling that some—and it is only some—couples go through prior to tying the knot?

Part of the power of sex—and possibly an important reason why, in 1 Corinthians 7, Paul tells married couples to have lots of it—is that the neurological impact of sex helps us instill and build intimacy with our partner. More intimacy leads to more and better sex, which in turn leads to even more intimacy. Being known and having a deep and meaningful connection is the foundation of a healthy marriage, and if we aren't cultivating that, it will lead to hurtful expressions of sexuality later. Relationship expert Dr. Sue Johnson reminds us of this: "We stray and have affairs not because we are all naturally inclined to have multiple mates but because our bond with our partner is either inherently weak or has deteriorated so far that we are unbearably lonely."[8]

It is crucial to help our teens think toward marriage in order to teach them a healthy view of sexuality for their lives in middle and high school, but also into adulthood.

MY PLAN

Start talking about sex earlier

Practically speaking, the advice I have most often given to youth workers and parents regarding talking to kids about sex is to start early. The sex talk shouldn't be just for high school students, but also middle schoolers and late elementary kids (fifth and sixth grade). The fact is that most parents come to these conversations much too late. Years ago, I did an informal survey with fourteen of my student leaders about sexuality and this point was driven home for me.[9]

- The average age that they first learned about sex was **nine years old**...and **only five** of them learned about it from an adult.

- The average age they learned about oral sex was **ten and a half years old**...and **none** learned about it from adult (unless you want to count the one who read about it in *Cosmo*).

- The average first time they heard about a peer engaging in sexual activity was at **twelve years old** (the **latest** was fourteen).[10]

- The average age that they got "the talk" from a parent was **twelve years old**...with three answering "**never**."

On average, their parents were three years too late to the conversation. From other statistics I have read regarding similar research on a broader scale, I would say this represents the typical scenario for many of our youth today. Ideally—and I acknowledge that this is next to impossible given our digital age—our youth should first be hearing and learning about sex from their parents and other trusted adults. The only way we can make that happen is to talk about it early.

Talk about sex often

We also need to talk about sex often. I have always made a point to have at least one week of our youth program year dedicated to the topic. And more often than not, I've done a four- to six-week series on dating, marriage, and sex every year.[11] Beyond the specific topical teaching, part of fostering an environment that makes teens feel safe to engage in open and honest dialogue about sex means that you open the door by bringing up the topic regularly.

One of the ways I have done this is by strategically using trips to start the conversation. I treat retreats and mission trips, especially late-night conversations in the dorms, as springboards to have casual conversations about sex and masturbation and honestly answer their questions, which I encourage them to ask. I've chosen to give my sex talk early on in the week of our annual mission trip, which brings about all sorts of questions and conversations that continue throughout our time together and sets a comfort level for more discussion back home.

Equip, engage, and encourage parents

I've already touched on this, but a major part of any plan to tackle the topic of sexuality needs to be equipping parents. In many ways, it's just as important to make space for open and honest communication with the parents you work with as it is with their teens. Many parents need to be told the truth about their kids and the sexually pervasive culture they are growing up in. I have broken the news to many parents that "yes, your thirteen-year-old is masturbating and most likely looking at porn." All of them thanked me after that conversation, and I was then able to partner with and guide them in dealing with reality, rather than pretending.

Every time you are doing a teaching or series on sex, it's important to make sure that detailed e-mails are going out to parents beforehand. You should be very clear about what will be discussed in your meetings and why you believe it is important. A key part of these communications should be encouraging parents to enter into conversations with their kids after your programs. Give them questions they can ask and tips on how to listen and get their teens to open up. I also committed to doing at least one parent workshop every year on the topic. This is one way of giving parents solid training on how to talk with their kids about sex. It's an uncomfortable subject for many parents, so part of your job is helping them get more comfortable, keeping in mind that many of them were not part of healthy parent-child conversations about sex in their own youth.

Foster a culture of vulnerability

When it comes to the adult leadership of your group, your plan should include fostering a culture of vulnerability. You don't want perfect adults and teens leading the conversation about sex. Rather than solely amplifying the voices of those who—seemingly, at least—have it all together, seek out and encourage leaders who will be honest about what they have learned about sex through their experiences and through Scripture. This will mean, in part, that your youth will hear from different voices, who should offer different perspectives. This helps teens wrestle with and think through a variety of views. I believe in nurturing a spirit of grace, where leaders are willing to admit struggles or difficulties, not in a "scare tactic" sense, but in an honest, relationally-driven way that aims simply to share the wisdom they have learned about the power of sex.

The unmarried woman who gets pregnant may be the perfect person to have on your youth ministry leadership team because she is honest and humble about her choices and what she is learning about God in the midst of her normal and imperfect life. The teenager who is struggling with an addiction to porn while trying to honor God with his or her sexuality could be the perfect role model to have on your student leadership team. When it comes to discipleship and leadership guidelines, we need to have policies and standards that deal with unhealthy and sinful behaviors, no matter what they are, and we also need to nurture a culture that allows people to be flawed humans who make mistakes, as we all are.

Teach teens to think critically about sex

The last and biggest aspect of my plan for tackling this topic with teenagers is that it isn't your job to get them to regurgitate a theology about sex or to parrot answers and views that you or their parents want them to have.[12] Your job is to teach them how to think critically about their sexuality. This means both how, if, and when they practice it, and why they believe what they believe about it. I would much rather have a teenager reach a different conclusion than me on sexual practices but be able to thoughtfully explain the reasons for their thinking than have that teenager agree with me but not be able to explain anything in depth when pressed with questions on why.

Encouraging teens to think critically and develop their own beliefs is the only way to guide them in the direction of owning their theology. Helping our youth do this gives them the chance to live out morals— morals they have fully thought through and decided to commit to on their own.

I seek to help teens think critically and own their beliefs in a number of ways:

First, when I do more of a teaching or workshop for teens, I always explicitly give them permission to disagree with me, and— importantly—I challenge them to actually do so. I tell them that they can interrupt me any time to ask questions and push back. I have often given out my cell number and told teens they can text questions if they don't want to raise their hands in front of everyone. I also always give out a resource list that has Scriptures they can explore, YouTube videos they can watch, or books they can read. I encourage teens not to take my experiences as gospel but to do the work themselves, digging into the Bible as well as scientific articles or books to explore the topic more deeply. I make myself available to them via text, on Facebook Messenger, or over a cup of coffee to discuss and debate as well.

Second, my preference in handling this topic is to do so in a discussion format, whether it's in a small group environment or it's facilitating a very interactive session in your large group meeting. Getting your teens to grapple with the Bible themselves and talk with one another is the best way I have found of helping them think more deeply about sex. Starting the conversation about sex can at first be a little slow and awkward, but in my experience once you establish that you are comfortable with the topic and the setting is safe for honest discussion, the conversation turns on like a fire hose.

Dialogue has also been the best way I have found to get teens to think about some of the negative aspects of sex: teen pregnancy, STIs, emotional challenges, etc. The teens we work with aren't naïve, and they aren't stupid. Once you have gone through your discussion, talking about what sex is and why it's so good from a scientific and theological standpoint, all you have to do is pose a question asking about the wisest ways to use our sexuality. Your teens will bring up everything else on their own. As they raise topics and voice opinions, encourage thoughtful conversation by asking who agrees or disagrees with each point that is shared. Structuring your discussion this way leaves the brunt of the message they hear from you and other adults as "Sex is good!" while still allowing youth to think through tough topics, striving to personally own and live out their sexuality in the best way possible.

The **third** element of my plan is the most difficult to carry out. Many teens have an expectation with church that at some point the pastor is going to wrap everything up with a little bow and tell them all the right answers. I try to avoid that as much as possible. Simply telling teens the exact things they should and shouldn't do robs them of any ownership of their beliefs and, in turn, of their behaviors. As I already stated, I don't think that is very effective. An honest dialogue about sex will leave teens wanting more when the conversation ends. I encourage them to keep wrestling, to keep asking questions, to read or research, and to engage in more conversations with their peers, with myself and other trusted adults, and with their parents.

FINAL THOUGHTS

Now please don't hear what I'm not saying. I am not saying to leave teens in a state of confusion or to tell them that sexual truth is all relative, that they can just do whatever feels right. Instead, it's the opposite. I want teens to walk out of the room hearing very clearly that God believes that sex is amazing and has designed it to be a spiritually and biologically powerful experience for us. When that is conveyed clearly, it becomes obvious to youth that something that powerful shouldn't be used in a thoughtless and carefree way. When teens walk out of the conversation thinking, processing, and wanting to go deeper, that is a key part of helping them develop a healthy and biblical view of sexuality that they can call their own.

RESPONSE

JOEL STEPANEK

Shame is a double-edged sword. In one regard, shame protects us from situations in which we may be hurt or feel vulnerable. As a child, I remember feeling a sense of shame when I saw pictures from a *Playboy* magazine. My conscience was signaling that I was approaching something sacred (the body) in a profane way. But shame can become distorted when we don't address it properly. Rather than recognizing that my shame in seeing those pictures was caused by encountering something good (a person) in a bad way, I simply thought the body, and subsequently sex, were bad things.

I identified with Jake's opening story. I think it is one many of us, especially in the Christian world, share. Many of us have negative attitudes toward sex that take years to work through, if we choose to work through them at all. I am in wholehearted agreement with him that the Christian church needs to do a much better job speaking honestly, positively, and openly about sex and sexuality.

Jake highlights something that's critically important. We must not use sexual education to make statements about sex being good within marriage—and then follow those statements with a list of "buts," where every problem, issue, or negative effect of sex is spoken of in an effort to encourage abstinence. This negative attitude toward sex, as Jake points out, not only shames young people but also elevates sexual sin above the level of any other sin.

In the chapter, Jake discusses Jesus's fulfillment of the law, and could easily incorporate Jesus's words on divorce in Matthew 19 to illustrate this kind of fulfillment of Mosaic Law (since Moses permitted divorce). I do, though, challenge Jake's application of Matthew 5:17-20, regarding which he writes, "What this means for Christ followers today is that Christ's death made the law completely irrelevant" and "it's impossible to completely follow the law." I agree with Jake that our faith cannot simply be lived out of fear of what may happen if we break the rules. At the same time, we also need to remember that Jesus, in the same Sermon on the Mount, calls us to "be perfect...as your heavenly Father is perfect." I think saying that the law is "irrelevant" is going a bit too far. Yes, we need to live beyond the requirements of the law because we are called to more—but Jake seems to imply that there is no way we can ever avoid sin. Our difference here is largely informed by our respective theological traditions. I believe that, with God's grace and a cooperation of the will, one could avoid sin and adhere to what Jesus calls us toward—though this path of perfection is only possible with God's grace, our growth in virtue, and diligence. But addressing the nuance of whether or not avoiding sin is impossible is, I think, important. For teenagers, what Jake suggests could easily seem like an "out," i.e., "Well, I'm going to sin anyway, so what is the point? Jesus still forgives me."

While I agree with much of what Jake writes, there are some areas where his argument could be stronger. First, in his discussion about the concept of marriage in Genesis not being tied to our religious ceremonies and liturgical expression of marriage, he misses the critical tie-in with Matthew 19:1-19, where Jesus specifically references the union of Adam and Eve as the prototype for marriage (and justification for a prohibition against divorce). Likewise, while Scripture may not lay out all of the instructions for marriage ceremonies, Scripture also doesn't lay out explicit guidelines for much of our modern day worship or sacramental action—though it does lay out the concepts and even the language we use. Second, the theological driver surrounding the "man-made" vs. "God-given" concepts of marriage ("biblically speaking, sex equals marriage") needs some bolstering since it is critical for his later argument. As it stands, it seems to imply that marriage, while good, may not necessarily be the only relationship where sex can be sacred rather than distorted.

Jake's ideas for working with teens are great, but again, are lacking in emphasizing what makes sex a good thing, because even in marriage sex can be distorted. I agree that we need to stop shaming teens who have had sex before marriage and must walk away from the "purity culture" that has formed. That said, we also need to challenge teens to strive for holiness, and I think Jake does a good job toeing that line. Where he misses the mark in his discussion of sex is in not emphasizing that it is designed to bring forward life. His emphasis on the unifying aspects, emotional aspects, and spiritual aspects are spot on—but throughout his discussion, the reality that sex is powerful because it can create new human life is lacking. If we are going to walk teenagers into an authentic understanding of sexuality, the dual purposes of sex (to be both unifying and procreative) must be emphasized equally. It is not enough to say that sex is powerful because two people become one flesh; we must also add that sex is powerful because through that union we, as humans, can also bring forward new life—life that has a soul and an eternal destiny to know, love, and serve God.

VIEW 2: EXPOSING YOUNG PEOPLE TO EXPLICIT TRUTH

JONATHAN MCKEE

She was barely twenty years old when I met her. Her two-year-old sat next to her, playing quietly with a stuffed SpongeBob, looking up at us with his big brown eyes.

"I just had no idea," she told me. "My parents never talked with me about it."

"Never?" I asked.

"Well, one day when I was like sixteen my mom told my dad, 'You better give her *the talk*.' My dad walked into my room and said, 'You know about sex, right?' I nodded. 'And you know not to do it, right?' I nodded again. And that was it!"

She was fifteen years old when she first became sexually active.

"I knew I wasn't supposed to 'do it,'" she said, "but I didn't really know much about 'doing it.' So whenever I was alone with a boy I did pretty much everything but 'it.'" She made little quote signs with her fingers.

"But once I started dating a guy seriously at seventeen," she continued, "we went further and further each time we were together. One night we were alone at his house and things got so heated it was impossible to stop. I had no idea what I was getting into."

She pulled her toddler up onto her lap and gave him a hug. "I can't say I regret him," she said, nodding toward her son. "But his dad made it clear that we were both mistakes, so I had to drop out of school, start working a minimum-wage job, and raise him by myself."

"I live in a studio apartment." Tears welled up in her eyes. "No one told me this is where I'd end up."

"What will you do differently," I asked, "raising your son?"

"Oh, trust me, we're going to talk about it," she said, kissing him on the forehead. "He's going to know what happens when two people get in a room alone. He's going to know everything. I want him to know the whole story."

The Talk

A few years ago when I was doing research for my parenting book, *More Than Just the Talk*, I interviewed dozens of young people like this young lady from churches and ministries scattered across the U.S. The one thing I asked them to do was this:

"Tell me about the conversations your parents had with you about sex."

The most common response I received was, literally, laughter. Not because the subject was awkward, but because…there was no *talk*. And if there was, it was once, it was awkward, and it wasn't very specific.

I think kids raised in the church almost have it worse than most. For some reason, many church parents seem to see "the talk" as something naughty. So they avoid it, or at least put it off until the child has a beard and a full-time job.

Most researchers in the field agree on one certainty: conversations about sex are vital. And, there *shouldn't* be just one talk. It should actually be an ongoing conversation. A few years ago the journal *Pediatrics* published a study entitled *Beyond the 'Big Talk*,'[1] encouraging parents to consider having repeated discussions with their children about many aspects of sex instead of just one big talk. The conclusion of the study was simple: "the more parents talked with their children, the closer their relationships." In fact, the relationship between parent and child really benefitted when the discussions "moved beyond 'safe' or impersonal subjects such as puberty, reproduction and sexually transmitted diseases to more private topics such as masturbation and how sex feels."

And that's where Christian parents shudder.

"I don't want to engage them in that kind of conversation. It might give them ideas."

So they're silent.

To me, the most intriguing element of talking with teenagers about sex is how often we *don't* talk with teenagers about sex.

Sure, youth leaders all dedicate one week annually to talking about sex and dating in youth group, or maybe even do a series over a few weeks, usually around Valentine's Day, with a creative title like "Waiting Before Mating." But then it's back to other topics that don't require a letter to parents, which, by the way, always triggers a number of moms and dads to keep their kids home that week because "Tyler isn't thinking about that yet."

Sadly, Tyler is fifteen, drowning in hormones, and whenever he catches a glimpse of the pink bra strap of the girl sitting in front of him in geometry his head explodes. If he's like most fifteen-year-olds, he's surrounded by sexually charged talk and imagery, but doesn't quite know what to do with the feelings that come along with them. He wouldn't dare tell Mom and Dad what he's experiencing, because *they're Mom and Dad!* And they don't feel the need to address the subject because they "don't really want to introduce something to him that he isn't already thinking about." So they just skip over the Tamar story in Genesis (and the story of the garden, and the Lot story, and the *other* Lot story…you get the idea).

Mom and Dad console themselves with the fact that they went through a (very tame) "purity" curriculum with Tyler three summers ago. Dad hit play on a CD and when it finished he asked, "Any questions?" Tyler had about 162 questions, but replied, "Nope."

Whew! Glad we don't have to talk about that anymore.

Forget the fact that Tyler is hearing dozens of "sex talks" each day, but from Drake, Ariana Grande, and that one really horny kid in P.E. class. But maybe, somehow, that *one talk* three years ago on Dad's boom box will remain resilient. (Hope that was a pretty potent talk!)

Yes, our culture typically refers to "the talk" is if it's singular, not an ongoing conversation.

"Have you had *the talk* with little Ezekiel yet?"

"No way. My little Ezekiel is homeschooled. He isn't even thinking about that stuff."

"Isn't Ezekiel seventeen?"

"Yes, but he is into other things, like fashion. In fact, sometimes he takes the J. C. Penney catalogue into the bathroom to browse through it for thirty minutes at a time."

And let's be honest. Today's teens have access to far beyond what's in a paper catalogue or magazine. A simple Google search will do. Not to mention Instagram and Snapchat, which provide stories from their favorite Kardashian and access to magazines like *Cosmo* that feature articles like "Learn How to Have an Orgasm Every Time." Meanwhile, Spotify is offering a steady stream of the top music, some of it shockingly explicit.

And if Mom or Dad *do* decide to have "the talk," it usually is that one-time talk. It's about body parts, it's vague, and it often doesn't convey much more than "just don't do it." And typically it doesn't answer the big questions their kids are afraid to ask, like…

- How do I know this ancient Bible is even right? I mean, didn't I read on the Internet that some book in the Bible says we can't even wear a shirt that's a cotton-polyester mix?

- Are you sure sex is really such a big deal? I mean, why would God create something so awesome and then just ban us from it? That sucks!

- If sex before marriage truly is wrong, can't I still have oral sex (and engage in a dozen other activities I don't really want to verbalize at the moment)?

- And what if I'm having same-sex attraction? Is that really wrong?

Mom and Dad typically aren't having *these* conversations.

But the entertainment media is.

The result?

The sources telling young people the truth about sex seem irrelevant or few and far between. The people who should be telling our kids about sex are often silent. But the voices telling our kids to gratify their immediate desires are loud and plentiful.

Looking for answers
So where do young people go with these important questions about sex and intimacy?

The little devices in their pockets have all the answers.

Siri, what does "getting top top by a thot thot" mean?

YouTube is another go-to source. If a girl searches "Should I Have Oral Sex?" she'll find a variety of videos to watch. One is from a very friendly little girl wearing glasses who will give advice about getting tested beforehand and reminds viewers that "you don't have to return the favor" when "someone goes south with their mouth." More is happening than just the video's content. On the side of the screen is a lineup of other recommended videos, like "8 Places that Men Like to Be Touched," or "Porn Stars Play 'Never Have I Ever,'" or even "6 Important Facts about Squirting."

Siri, what is 'squirting'?

And Mom thought the Tamar story would distract?

A 2018 study on teens and social media[2] revealed that ninety-five percent of teens have access to a smartphone, and ninety-seven percent are on social media. And on average, kids get their first smartphone at age 10.3.[3] Most parents have no clue what their kids are accessing with these devices.

So?

What does this have to do with young people's understanding of sex and intimacy?

Everything. Boys are growing up with more distractions than ever before, and girls are growing up thinking they have to be as sexy as Kendall and as popular as Kylie. The messages are pretty consistent:

Guys: be badass, do whatever feels right in the moment, enjoy girls— who are objects, by the way—and smoke a little sum-something if you're too stressed by it all.

Girls: be sexy, lose control, please men, but be strong and independent (and a little slutty).

So Justin continues to click on racy pics and videos every night. Emily turns to Instagram for approval, knowing that the sexier, the better. Of course, Mom and Dad don't know about these posts. Emily has two Insta accounts—one for parents, and one for her friends.

All of this illustrates something fundamental: today's young people are looking for deep fulfillment. But when they look for it in the casual sex and "look at me" identities they've been sold, they are unable to find it. Is it any surprise that we're seeing unprecedented rates of depression, anxiety, and suicide among teens?[4]

So what's the solution?

Here's where I will tip my cards to you, the reader.

MY ASSUMPTIONS AND THEOLOGICAL ANCHORS

In a world where young people are searching in all the wrong places for fulfillment, it's pretty obvious that what's needed is much bigger than a sex talk. We have an incredible opportunity to introduce young people to a relationship with Jesus that changes everything. Jesus gives purpose, identity, and the strength to endure tough times. (And for many young people today, middle school and high school are synonymous with "tough times.")

Here's where I will insert, almost as an aside, that some of the most effective ministries I've seen at reaching youth who are blatantly sexually promiscuous are ministries that focus on exposing people to Christ and letting his redemptive work take place in their lives. This isn't to say that they don't ever talk about God's design for sex and intimacy—they do. But they don't begin there. They begin with God's love for them and how they could have a relationship with him through Jesus. Then they let the Spirit do his work in their lives as they dive into the Word and learn more about him.

So as we look at the biblical basis for teaching on sex and intimacy, I preface it with the notion that we don't need to wave these theological points as a banner (there is more on this in the section of this chapter called My Plan). In fact, whenever I typically engage today's young people in conversations about sex and intimacy, I start with research and reasoning, showing them how monogamous relationships make sense. Once they grasp that, I introduce them to the author of true monogamy.

So what are the theological anchors that inform my views on biblical monogamy?

First, I see the Bible as the infallible Word of God. I won't spend any time arguing the trustworthiness of the Bible and its teachings here. Feel free to read books like *The New Evidence That Demands a Verdict* (Josh McDowell) or *The Case for Christ* (Lee Strobel) or even *Biblical Preaching* (Haddon Robinson).

But how we approach and read that Word is also important. We don't—or, at least, we *shouldn't*—come to Scripture with ideas about what we want it to say, and then look for verses that confirm what we expect to see. Instead we should come to Scripture prayerfully, asking God to reveal to us what the text says. And context is everything. In the same way that we wouldn't read the second part of Act 3 of *Romeo and Juliet* and draw conclusions without reading the rest of the play, we need to carefully interpret Scripture within the greater context of the grand redemptive storyline of the Bible.

Why is this important? Because many people approach Scripture as a smorgasbord. They take what they like and leave what they don't.

It's not hard to understand why this happens. It's difficult for someone today, with no biblical training, to read Leviticus for the first time and understand the laws that seem so weird. It's much easier to make sense of what we read when we understand a little bit about Scripture in the big picture sense, like how it addresses moral law, civil law, and ceremonial law. Moral law, as found in the Bible, is unchanging, but civil and ceremonial laws in the Bible are often for that specific time. Sure, it would be nice if sometimes the writer of a book of the Bible would say, "Hey, this is one of those unchanging moral laws—don't commit adultery." And then maybe, "Since you guys don't have any policemen on patrol right now, here's what you need to do if your dog wanders into your neighbor's yard and attacks his goat..."

That's why an understanding of the grand storyline of Scripture is so helpful. Let's take the topic of adultery, for instance. You read about God's original design of man and woman becoming one flesh. Then you read as God emphasizes the Ten Commandments to Moses and those commandments include not committing adultery. And then still you read when Jesus says (I'm paraphrasing from Matthew 5 here), "You've heard it said, 'Do not commit adultery,' but now I say…" The repetition is apparent. What's being taught is emphasized so often, it's obviously pretty important. The message is unchanging throughout Scripture.

Let's take a quick peek at what Scripture tells us about God's design, which will help us understand what we need to communicate to young people today.

MY PRIORITIES

What's most important for us to communicate?
A quick reminder, before we dive into God's design: remember, you don't have to cover this all in one talk.

In fact, we need to expunge the phrase "the talk" from our ministries and our culture.

Knowing none of this fits neatly into a one-time occurrence of "the talk" takes the pressure off a little bit. It's pretty difficult to communicate God's entire design for sex and intimacy in one thirty-minute session on Valentine's Day. It's a silly notion. Here's where we need to take Yoda's advice: "You must unlearn what you have learned."

So breathe a sigh of relief. You don't need to communicate this all in one night! Research even shows that far more effective than a one-time "talk" is having an ongoing conversation.

Think of the pressure this takes off of moms and dads when their third grade boy asks his father, "Dad, why does my penis get big like this?"

Historically, this is where parents felt the need to sit little Christopher down and teach him every last detail about sex. This happens with girls, too. Often "the talk" has happened whenever little Christina first learns about menstruation. This is the impetus to teach kids everything they'll ever hear from their parents about sex and their reproductive systems. That's intimidating. And it can be scary for parents, so much so that they may just avoid the whole thing altogether. My daughter actually had a friend in middle school who began menstruating and thought she was dying—*because her parents had never taught her about that!*

We don't have to cover everything from pubic hair to oral sex in one conversation! There should be many, many conversations.

So what's the most important thing to communicate?

Let's go back to the beginning. Like…"in the beginning."

God's design

It's the big picture that, sadly, most young people never hear about. In the beginning we see God's amazing creation. A naked man was walking around the garden and God said, "It's not good for the man to be alone" (Genesis 2:18).

This is where the story gets pretty good.

Poof!

A naked woman.

God created the perfect complement. The woman was like the man, but different. A perfect fit. Like a right hand joining together perfectly with a left.

But it gets better. God says, "Multiply."

Adam doesn't argue.

Then Scripture tells us, "That is why a man leaves his father and mother and is united to his wife, and they become one flesh. Adam and his wife were both naked, and they felt no shame" (Genesis 2:24-25).

Genesis gives us a glimpse of God's remarkable design: husband and wife, beginning their own life together, "united" and "one flesh."

When man and woman marry they become one unit. Bonded. Connected to form something that isn't supposed to be separated. The term "one flesh" articulates this intrinsic connection.

Some may argue that this Scripture from Genesis is old and outdated. I've heard people say, "We're a New Testament church. That's Old Covenant" (which actually reveals their lack of understanding of the New Testament). But even if that were so, we have to ask ourselves: if the Old Covenant was strict and the New Covenant was more lax, then how come when it comes to certain subjects like sex, Jesus was actually more conservative than the religious leaders of the day?

Consider Matthew 5:27-30 in the Sermon on the Mount.

> "You have heard that it was said, 'You shall not commit adultery.' But I tell you that anyone who looks at a woman lustfully has already committed adultery with her in his heart. If your right eye causes you to stumble, gouge it out and throw it away. It is better for you to lose one part of your body than for your whole body to be thrown into hell. And if your right hand causes you to stumble, cut it off and throw it away. It is better for you to lose one part of your body than for your whole body to go into hell."

Jesus didn't backpedal at all. He didn't say, "Hey, this was the old law, and that's gone. Sleep with anyone you like." He did the exact opposite. He expanded on the old law, letting it be known that what matters is not simply our actions, but our thoughts behind those actions. Yikes!

Even more intriguing is his interaction with the Pharisees in Matthew 19 (and Mark 10):

> Some Pharisees came to him to test him. They asked, "Is it lawful for a man to divorce his wife for any and every reason?"

> "Haven't you read," he replied, "that at the beginning the Creator 'made them male and female,' and said, 'For this reason a man will leave his father and mother and be united to his wife, and the two will become one flesh'? So they are no longer two, but one flesh. Therefore what God has joined together, let no one separate."

This passage brings us back to that original Genesis account. Jesus reminds us of God's perfect design of male and female, who leave mom and dad and become "one flesh." And then he emphasizes the permanence of this true monogamous relationship. It's one that shouldn't be separated.

The intriguing thing is how much science supports the bonding that takes place in a monogamous relationship. Take oxytocin, for example. When you study the human body, you'll find that the body releases a powerful hormone called oxytocin when you hug or kiss someone you really care about. It's not just sex that releases this hormone, it's intimate touch. Some actually call this hormone the bonding hormone or the cuddle hormone. And yes, it's released big time during sexual activity. Scientists who do research on "pair bonding" find that monogamous people and animals produce huge amounts of this hormone over time. These bonded couples even have increased levels of pleasure boosting hormones when they simply see or think about their partner.[5]

This is why the pain of a breakup is so great. Think of the thousands of songs written about the kind of hurt that comes with the end of a relationship. The more we bond with someone, sharing the most intimate parts of ourselves, the more it rips us apart when we separate.

It's almost as if the guy behind the design of all this didn't want us to make that sexual connection unless we meant to stay together, eh? When we don't, we're unjoining something God joined.

This is why we need to be proactive about sharing God's design with young people. The world is quick to tell us, "Do whatever feels right in the moment." What the world neglects to share are the consequences of living that way.

It makes sense when you think about it. Who wants to listen to that song?

"You looked so good out there on the dance floor. But I refrained from engaging you in sexual activity because I knew it would only cheapen our relationship and the bond we could have if we showed patience and self-control and waited until marriage."

That one would never hit the charts.

But interestingly enough, the music charts do actually reflect some of these same truths. Because as often as music talks about "doing whatever you like," music also reveals something undeniably real that everyone knows well:

Hurt.

My coworker David R. Smith and I have observed this reality in our youth culture research over the last fifteen years. Most popular music falls into one of two categories:

- **Do whatever you like.** You'll hear this expressed in many ways: let go; lose control; I can't stop; it feels so right; live for the moment; who cares; it's what I want; live like there's no consequence; we ain't ever getting older!

- **Regret.** Countless examples: it hurts; you wrecked me; you broke my heart; you tore me open; I'm devastated, hopeless, alone, crying for help; no one is there; I'm in pain, damaged, suicidal; drinking it away; drowning the pain; wishing it were different; trying to forget; I'm lonely!

Hmmmmmm.

Is there a chance that when we "live for the moment" and "lose control" it results in "hurt" and a "broken heart" that lead us to feel "alone" and "suicidal" so we self-medicate by "drinking" to "drown the pain"? It's like sometimes the world just doesn't want to put two and two together.

It's logical if you think about it, though. If we live for temporary thrills then that's exactly what we get: fun for a limited amount of time. It's the marshmallow test on steroids. Do you want one marshmallow now or two marshmallows in five minutes? Do you want thrilling sex now, or the most fulfilling sex for the rest of your life?

If we live *carefree*, most of us eventually discover we do *care*, and it wasn't *free*.

Surprisingly, that's what many people discuss when they compare monogamy to promiscuity.

Monogamy

I find it intriguing how little conversation there is about monogamy. It's an essential practice to understand. When I'm talking with young people, I like to bring it up with a question:

> *What's more satisfying: sleeping with whoever you want, or saving yourself for one person for life?*

This term *saving yourself* draws from our prior discussion about delayed gratification. What if we want the marshmallow now?! Isn't it more fun to sleep with whoever we want? Monogamy sounds boring, right?

Have you ever compared monogamy with promiscuity?

In my book for young people, *Sex Matters* (Chapter 1: Why Wait?),[6] I actually share research from a variety of secular sources, including the *Journal of Psychology*, comparing individuals who were promiscuous to those who chose monogamy. The results of those studies are eye-opening.

You might surmise that those who do whatever they like (more like "whoever they like") would be happier. But the opposite is true. In fact, according to most studies, the more sexual partners someone had, the less satisfied they were with their current sexual relationship.

Think about this for a moment. Most people who were sexually promiscuous regret it, as opposed to looking back at it with favor.

Wouldn't this be good information for young people to hear?

Again, different young people will respond to different studies and different examples. That's why it's helpful when you don't have to cram everything into one talk. And one of the talks I find essential is a conversation about covenant vs. consumer relationships.

Covenant relationships

I've found that one of the most convincing cases by far for God's design is the one communicated by pastor Tim Keller (whose core audience, by the way, is millennials in New York City—not exactly a bunch of conservatives in the Bible Belt).

In Keller's book *The Meaning of Marriage*,[7] he introduces the concept of covenant relationships versus consumer relationships. Our culture seems especially attracted to consumer relationships. A consumer relationship is based on a simple concept: "If you keep doing your part, I'll keep doing my part." It's conditional. If my spouse changes her "product quality" (like she gets less attractive, or doesn't provide enough sex) then I'll go find a better product, like any consumer would.

People tend to hide blemishes and insecurities in consumer relationships. Why? "If he or she sees my flaws, he or she might reject me."

A covenant relationship, however, is not based on whether the other person delivers the goods. A covenant relationship says, "I love you regardless." The unconditional love in covenant relationships allows the people in them to be truly known.

God uses marriage as an example of how he loves us as his bride, unconditionally (Ephesians 5). I'm sure glad God doesn't have a consumer relationship with me. He would have traded me in long ago!

Ask any woman which kind of relationship she would prefer: the one where she has to measure up each day, or the one where it's clear she is known and loved? Ask any man the same thing.

Who wants to live in a relationship where fear is always simmering on the back burner?

Every once in a while, pop culture reveals the desire humans have to find "the one" (in other words, to settle with one person for life). I can't help but think of the movie *Crazy Stupid Love* (written by *This is Us* screenwriter Dan Fogelman), starring Ryan Gosling, Emma Stone, and Steve Carell.[8]

At first the movie appears to be morally bankrupt. Cal (Carell) begins going to a singles bar after his wife asks him for a divorce. There he meets Jacob (Gosling), who teaches him how to pick up girls and bring them home. After all, Jacob is a sex machine. He literally leaves with a different girl each night.

But Jacob meets Hannah (Stone) and his world is rocked. Next thing he knows he wants to enter a monogamous relationship with Hannah, abandoning the very promiscuous lifestyle he was advocating to Cal. The story has some creative twists and turns. It's a great movie!

Think of how many cherished love stories end with two people committing to "for better or worse, 'til death do us part." They're revealing a desire held deep within our being.

It's almost like we were designed for that kind of relationship from the beginning.

So how can we actually communicate all of these truths to young people today?

MY PLAN

How I talk about sex

One thing we need to consider is what we're communicating about sex and intimacy—even when we're not overtly communicating about sex and intimacy. For example, how do we treat people who are living out the world's values?

We can have the best "sex talk" in youth ministry history, but if we treat "sinners" like lesser beings, then they won't hear a word we say (dare I say, we'll be a resounding gong or clanging cymbal, 1 Corinthians 13).

Jesus obviously lived this perfectly, because the more people were perceived as sinners, the more they wanted to be with Jesus. Jesus had a presence about him that said, "I won't hold your past against you. I care too much about your future." We never see Jesus compromise this theology. He just seeped love through every pore, caring for people like no other.

So the first question we might need to ask ourselves is, *What do other people see when they look at my life and my ministry?* Do they see Christlike empathy and compassion? Or do they witness something judgmental and abrasive?

When during my research I was interviewing dozens of ministries about reaching out to young people identifying as LGBTQ, I encountered a conservative youth pastor who had a dynamic ministry serving and caring for this group of young people. He told me, and I quote, "I've looked at Scripture countless times trying to find if there's a way that we can tell kids that homosexual relationships are no problem. It's just not there. But that doesn't stop us from reaching young people who identify as LGBTQ."

This young pastor's ministry has a reputation in the community for creating a safe place for anyone identifying as LGBTQ. In fact, he's had people at other conservative churches blame him for being soft on the issue.

"These other ministries never ask me what I believe," he told me. "They just assume since I am hanging out with gay kids and transgender youth that I somehow am giving them a stamp of approval."

I guess those churches missed some of the stories about Jesus, like Matthew 9:9-13, when Jesus has dinner at the house of Matthew the tax collector.

In fact, once a hate group came to his town to protest people identifying as LGBTQ. This pastor made up buttons that read "Loved by God" and gave them to all the youth in his ministry to wear and pass out. Teenagers all over the high school campus wore them that day.

The funny thing is, every single one of these young people identifying as LGBTQ knows where he stands theologically. But he doesn't feel the need to wear it on his vest, like, "I love you… but you know you're a sinner, right?" Whenever he encounters a passage that deals with God's plan for sex and intimacy, or "our identity in Christ," he teaches it as written.

And they listen.

He's earned the right to be heard, because he's shown them unconditional love and support.

Communicating God's message of love and truth starts with us living out love and truth.

But this doesn't mean we don't ever speak on an issue. Far from it. Jesus definitely wasn't afraid to tell the truth, even when it wasn't politically correct. He wasn't necessarily winning any friends when he told the crowds, "wide is the gate and broad is the road that leads to destruction, and many enter through it. But small is the gate and narrow the road that leads to life, and only a few find it" (Matthew 7:13-14).

So how do we communicate the message of truth in a world so comfortable with lies?

Know your audience

We can take a lesson from the apostle Paul when he engaged a group of people who were comfortable with almost every belief they came across. (Sound familiar?) I'm referring to the people of Athens in Acts 17, who had so many gods in their city, they each had a "coexist" sticker on the back of their chariot.

When Paul addressed them, he didn't start barking out judgment against their idolatry (even though the passage says it distressed him greatly). Instead, he used those very idols and words from the pagan poets as his starting point for his discussion about truth. He basically said, "Hey Athenians, I noticed you guys are very religious—I saw all your idols. You even had one dedicated to 'an unknown god.' Hey, I know who this 'unknown god' is that you've been worshipping all along! He's not made of bronze or stone—he's the creator of the entire universe. Let me tell you more about him."

Instead of *overreacting* about their idolatry, he began *interacting* with it, using their idolatry as a springboard for meaningful conversation.

If only we were so shrewd.

We need to navigate discussions about God's design for sex and intimacy wisely in this tumultuous climate, for two reasons:

1. Many people who use the label "Christian" don't represent Christ very well. This ruins it for those of us who truly believe Christ's teaching and are allowing him to transform our imperfect lives. Churches like Westboro Baptist (the "God hates fags" church) give Christians a bad name. Like when *Duck Dynasty's* Phil Robertson was asked, "What in your mind is sinful?" and he responded, "Start with homosexual behavior and just morph out from there."[9] (And within a year the show's ratings dropped off a cliff.) Why not answer, "Start with me. I'm the perfect example of someone who needs Jesus badly." But these public "Christian" figures have only catalyzed people to become skeptical of "Christian" teaching.

2. In a "do what's right for you" world, people don't like messages of "our choices have repercussions."

So we need to enter into these conversations discerningly. We can't just say, "The Bible says…" and expect people to pull up a chair, eager to hear God's unchanging truth.

So begin with their culture.

Not long ago I spoke at a public school assembly. In the Billboard Top 10 at the time was a song titled *No Limits* by a bunch of rappers, including Cardi B, A$AP Rocky, and G-Eazy. The chorus of this delightful little ditty simply repeats the line, "Ayy, yeah, f**k with me and get some money."

Later in this song G-Eazy brags:

> *Man, this year, I had 300 one-night stands*
> *Keep a Costco pack of rubbers in my nightstand…*

I joked with the audience that this sounded like the setup for a great math problem for homework that night—and then I took them to the CDC web page on STDs on the big screen, right there in the assembly hall.

Yes: we turned to research.

Research
I can't begin to tell you how effective presenting research is.

Why?

Because none of these teens have likely ever been on the CDC website. And even though it's sort of "academic," it's about sex! And who doesn't want to hear about sex?

The CDC web page gives all kinds of interesting facts about condom effectiveness and STDs. It doesn't take but a few clicks to be staring at the exact numbers on how effective condoms are against pregnancy and sexually transmitted infections. I joked with the teens about G-Eazy's "300 one-night stands."

> *Perhaps G-Eazy's physician should warn him by showing him some simple math. Let's start with his chance of getting one of these "one-night stands" pregnant, or to put it in language he might listen to, "paying child support!" If G-Eazy were to simply flip over that condom box on the nightstand he would read that condoms are 98 percent effective against pregnancy. So statistically, if Mr. "G" is sleeping with 300 different girls annually, then he will get six girls pregnant each year.*

> *That's a lot of child support!*

> *I don't think that was the intention when they sang the chorus, "f**k with me and get some money," but it's rather ironic.*

Then I took this group of young people to the CDC's web page about STD prevention,[10] and told them that even if G-Eazy ignores the CDC's advice that "the most reliable way to avoid infection is abstinence," followed by "reducing the number of sex partners" (whoops and whoops), then he might click over to the STD Fact Sheet page[11] where he can find helpful information on the STDs that are plaguing this country. For example, the most common STD, the human papillomavirus (HPV). The first sentence on the HPV and Men fact sheet reads:

> *Nearly all sexually active people will get human papillomavirus (HPV) at some time in their life if they don't get the HPV vaccine.*[12]

Wow! "Nearly all." How's that for a percentage.

Think about this. I haven't even opened a Bible and they just saw compelling secular research literally stating that abstinence is "the most reliable way to avoid infection."

Research can be powerful.

Again, no one ever goes over this stuff with young people.

I keep it short and choose a few compelling facts. Research speaks volumes.

But some young people don't really respond to research, so I also appeal to their ability to reason.

Reasoning

The cool thing about God's design is it just makes sense (which is why Tim Keller's consumer vs. covenant relationship example is so strong).

For years I've used this example when speaking to teens about sex. I simply tell the young people listening to close their eyes and picture something.

> *I want you to picture this world for a minute. Picture it exactly how you see it every day. Picture the things you find beautiful and the things you enjoy. What makes you laugh? What makes you smile? But let's be realistic. Let's also recognize some of the pain in this world: wars, hunger, sickness, brutality, death…the list goes on. This is the world we live in.*

Now I want you to make one small adjustment to this image, one little tweak to change your picture. Imagine the world exactly like it is now, but with one exception: for some reason, everyone in the entire world believes God's plan for sex and marriage and stays true to their one spouse for life.

The world still has suicide, crime, high school dropouts, and all other kinds of pain and hurt. If you ride your bike to the grocery store and leave it out front unlocked, it will be gone within five minutes because people still steal things in this world.

But even with all this pain and hurt, imagine that, for some unknown reason, every single person believes God's plan to wait until marriage for sex, and no one performs any sexual activity outside of the marriage relationship. No one lusts after anyone else, and once they get married they love each other and stay committed to their spouse, enjoying a sexual intimacy, just the two of them, for the rest of their lives.

Picture this world.

- *For starters, in this world Dad doesn't trade in his wife for a younger version.*
- *This is a world with no dads cheating on moms, or moms cheating on dads.*
- *There are no painful family splits because couples love each other and stay committed to each other.*
- *This is a world with no pornography, because no one is lusting and no one would pose for sexual pictures for that purpose.*
- *This is world with no prostitution, because sex is only for marriage.*
- *This is a world with no pedophiles (people who sexually abuse children), no molestation, and no sexual abuse of any kind, because, again, sex is only between a husband and wife in the intimacy of marriage.*

- *There aren't any "Who's Your Daddy" reality TV shows, and probably no one has any idea what a Kardashian is.*
- *This is a world with no STDs. No AIDS would be transmitted sexually, no gonorrhea, no herpes, no syphilis.*
- *This is a world with no chlamydia, the asymptomatic STD that often leads to pelvic inflammatory disease and eventually infertility problems in women.[13]*
- *This is a world with no HPV (the papillomavirus), which is the leading cause of cervical cancer in women.[14]*
- *This is a world with very few abortions, because eighty-three percent of abortions are performed out of wedlock.[15]*
- *This is a world with no rape.*
- *This is a world with no sex slavery.*

…the list goes on. All this if people just trusted God in that one area of their lives.

Imagine if they trusted him in everything.

Then I simply say, "Let me ask you—does God's way sound so bad?"

If I'm at a public school assembly I can paint this same picture by talking about monogamy and asking, "what if everyone waited for one person and stuck with that one person for life?" It's tricky to navigate, but I basically paint the same picture without telling them who the artist is.

In other contexts, if I'm allowed, I introduce them to the artist.

Scripture

I've actually taken heat from some conservatives about how I wait to bring up Scripture until last. But I study youth culture for a living and I know how much our culture values—or actually, how much our culture *doesn't* value—Scripture. I find it much more powerful to first show the research and reasoning, and once they're all nodding their heads, I introduce them to the Creator behind this perfect design.

I typically start with Genesis, in the beginning, using humor about the naked man in the garden and God making the naked woman, and man saying, "This is good!"

Then I often go to Proverbs 5:18-23, a very relevant passage for young people today.

> May your fountain be blessed,
> and may you rejoice in the wife of your youth.
> A loving doe, a graceful deer—
> may her breasts satisfy you always,
> may you ever be intoxicated with her love.
> Why, my son, be intoxicated with another man's wife?
> Why embrace the bosom of a wayward woman?
>
> For your ways are in full view of the Lord,
> and he examines all your paths.
> The evil deeds of the wicked ensnare them;
> the cords of their sins hold them fast.
> For lack of discipline they will die,
> led astray by their own great folly.

This passage preaches itself to guys. *Enjoy your wife's breasts, but not another woman's breasts. Why would you enjoy another woman's breasts? For what you do is in full view of God. Why be ensnared by this?*

But it's a message so relevant to both guys *and* girls about how a loving God created the gift of sex for us to actually *enjoy*. Think of the relevant small group questions you could provide for this passage.

- What does God tell these men to rejoice in? Why?
- What does he tell them to be satisfied with? Why do you think he's giving this advice?
- Does God want us to enjoy sex with the one we marry?
- What does he warn us about embracing? What is "the bosom"?
- Why *shouldn't* men enjoy other women's breasts?

- What do our evil deeds do to us?
- What are some common ways we get ensnared by sexual temptation today?
- What is a lack of discipline when it comes to sexual temptation?
- What does it mean to be led astray? What might that look like?
- What is one thing you can learn from this passage?
- How can you apply this to your life this week?

Again, it's difficult to cover all these concepts in one talk. But that's okay. It's better in a series of talks. In these talks I like to answer key questions like, "How do I know God's way is best?" "How far can I go—in other words, is oral sex okay?" "What about pornography?"[16]

Testimony

In any talk I like to finish with a story that helps illustrate the point. Sometimes the most compelling way to do this is to have someone you know share his or her story.

Testimonies are powerful. Sometimes even if teens didn't listen to the research, didn't buy into the reasoning, and didn't connect with the Scripture, they still might respond to a person who shares testimony of something that happened to them. Don't underestimate the power of a story.

I'll never forget Angelica's story.

FINAL THOUGHTS

Angelica is a youth worker working with a pretty rough group of kids in Texas. I've heard her share her story and not only is she very open about her own mistakes, she's proactive about connecting teen girls with positive adult role models.

Angelica grew up in a Christian home and heard many times that she should wait for sex until marriage. Her parents were very open about it and she heard the talk at youth group literally every year from sixth grade to twelfth.

But this Christian upbringing didn't totally shelter her from outside influences. Angelica went to public school, and many of her friends slept around. She listened to the music everyone else did, watched the same shows on Netflix, but despite these environmental influences, resolved to save sex for marriage. In fact, at age sixteen she got a purity ring.

Then she went off to a Christian college.

In college Angelica met a boy who was also raised in the church. He was everything she dreamed of. The two dated for months and had several "laying down the boundaries" conversations about waiting for sex until marriage.

Soon they talked about actually getting married. They didn't officially get engaged, but they definitely saw a wedding in their future, perhaps after they graduated together. It wasn't long before they found themselves casually saying, "When we get married…"

And that's when it happened.

One night when they were alone they decided, "Why not? We're going to get married anyway." And so the two of them made love. One time turned into two, and soon they were sleeping together regularly.

A year later the relationship took a bad turn and they broke up. The breakup devastated Angelica. It ripped her world apart.

Angelica eventually emerged from this situation hurt—and a little wiser. Now she shares her story with young people.

"I had heard the lecture a million times. 'Don't have sex until you're married.' But I thought, 'Hey, I'm going to marry this guy!'"

She goes on. "I never even allowed myself to consider, 'What if I *don't* marry this guy?' Right? I mean, who wants to think negative vibes like that?"

But the most interesting thing about her story is what she learned about *intimacy*.

"I always thought of sex and the importance of waiting all about the sexual act. What I didn't understand was the incredible connection that happens when two people join together so intimately. It bonds you in ways unimaginable. And if you happen to dissolve that relationship, severing that bond is an excruciatingly painful experience!"

Sadly, it took trial and error for Angelica to learn how sacred God's design for sex and intimacy really is. And when those deep-rooted connections are cut, there's a whole lot of hurt. We're talking like an Adele album of hurt!

If only someone had talked with Angelica about that.

But God has an amazing way of using our blunders for good. And now Angelica is using her own life lessons to help others.

I love what Angelica is doing. Today's youth workers could learn a lot from two aspects of Angelica's ministry:

1. She recognizes the essential need for ongoing conversations with young people about sex and intimacy. For Angelica, this is more than just one talk. This is adults connecting with teens in small groups and one-on-one, and being available for ongoing faith conversations.

This is youth ministry 101. It's mentoring 101. Discipleship 101. In fact, Kara Powell and few others at Fuller Seminary, in their Sticky Faith research, concluded that "Among 13 different ways adults support high school kids, two variables stood out as significantly related to sticky faith over time: feeling sought out by adults and feeling like those adults 'helped me to realistically apply my faith to my daily life.'"[17]

Angelica understands the importance of adults seeking out young people and engaging them in faith conversations.

"When I was sixteen I would have loved to have had someone to talk with," Angelica told me. "I didn't have anyone. But now I can be that person for others."

2. Angelica isn't just teaching biology, and she isn't just reading verses to young people about "fleeing sexual immorality." She's providing them with the entire picture of God's design for sex and intimacy, something no one ever told her.

In a world so overflowing with messages of "no consequences" and "live for today," many young people are ready to hear the truth about what happens when we wake up tomorrow.

How can you begin engaging young people in these—plural—conversations?

RESPONSE

JEN BRADBURY

Where Jonathan and I agree is that adults and, in particular, parents need to be engaged with teens in ongoing conversations with young people about sex. These conversations need to be rooted in Scripture so that teens understand God's design for sex and relationships.

I'm not, however, convinced that following Jonathan's plan will enable teens to understand "the entire picture of God's design for sex and intimacy." While Jonathan's plan might convince teens that men and women are "the perfect complement" to one another, it won't necessarily equip them to honor God—or even their partner—in their relationships with one another. While it will teach teens that sex is an important, expected part of marriage, it won't instill in them the importance of consent (even within marriage). While it might convince teens that waiting will guarantee them the "most fulfilling sex for the rest of your life," it won't prepare them to deal with the disappointment that comes when it isn't.

While CDC statistics might scare teens into remaining virginal until marriage, they won't prepare them to form a sexual ethic that will sustain them through their formative teenage years, single adult years, and into married life. Scare tactics might succeed at getting teens to say no to sex for a while, but they won't prevent teens from going farther than they'd like in a heated moment with someone they love and respect.

And that's just it. Even though Jonathan seems to think that we have to convince teens that monogamous relationships make sense, I'd argue that teens *want* to be in monogamous relationships. They just define them differently than he does. While Jonathan's definition of monogamy implies marriage, to today's teens, monogamy is having a sexual relationship with *one* partner they're not necessarily married to.

Because of these differing definitions, Jonathan falsely pits monogamy against sexual promiscuity. But in the sixteen years I've been a youth pastor, I haven't seen many teens struggle with being sexually promiscuous. I have, however, counseled plenty of teens who have wanted to have sex with the *one* person they're committed to. *That's the greatest temptation when it comes to sex for Christian teens, not randomly hooking up with strangers at a party.* Unfortunately, since buying condoms or securing birth control shows an intent to have sex that they don't want to express, when Christian teens find themselves in that moment they're often unprepared, making it far more likely that they'll become the statistics that well-intentioned youth workers like Jonathan have spent years scaring them about.

As youth workers and Christ-followers, it's possible for us to talk about condoms and birth control while still affirming that sex matters, that it deeply bonds people and shouldn't be taken lightly. Doing so acknowledges the real, complex world in which we live. Acknowledging the complexity of our world prepares teens to honor God and others with their bodies far more than imagining a world where "everyone in the entire world believes God's plan for sex and marriage and stays true to their one spouse for life."

Such a vision—while compelling—is dangerous because it can cause teens to falsely believe that the good news of Jesus applies only to some pie-in-the-sky fantasy world. In reality, the gospel applies to the real world in which teens actually live—one in which STDs, rape, sexual harassment, divorce, and abuse all exist.

By definition, the gospel is good news (and if it's not, it's not the gospel). Part of the good news of the gospel is that sex *is* good.

So are we.

And our teens.

That good news gets lost in Jonathan's plan because it focuses on how awful sex is before marriage but how amazing it is afterward. That doesn't make sense to teens who wonder how sex can be sinful until a pastor declares a couple wed.

Sex *is* good because God created it that way. That's part of God's "whole story" for sex and intimacy, which isn't as black and white as Jonathan makes it out to be. It's complex. But then, so are God and Scripture.

That's why, as youth workers and parents, we need to talk with teens about the complex "truth" about sex. We need to teach teens God's "whole story" for sex and intimacy, including the parts that make us uncomfortable. God's whole story for sex includes marriage. But it also includes Scripture passages that feature the patriarchs of our faith committing adultery and rape. It includes stories that showcase God's forgiveness and redemption as well as teachings that rail against sexual immorality—alongside a whole host of other wrongs.

In his chapter, Jonathan reminds us that "Jesus was actually more conservative than the religious leaders of the day." Jesus was also less legalistic, more relational, and more forgiving than the religious leaders. We should be too.

So, let's stop expecting teens to merely remain virgins until they marry and instead start trusting them to live in holiness and honor in every period of their lives. Let's equip them to do so by exploring Scripture (even the complex, messy parts) and teaching them to develop a whole-person sexual ethic that enables them to love God, themselves, and others both inside and outside of the bedroom.

When that happens, we won't have to imagine a world in which there are fewer affairs, STDs, and sex-based crimes. We'll be living in one.

VIEW 3: DEVELOPING A SEXUAL ETHIC

JEN BRADBURY

The day I started my first job in youth ministry, my boss walked into my office, threw a curriculum on my desk, and said, "We need you to lead this at the fall confirmation retreat." I looked down, saw the word "sex," and only then realized that I was being voluntold to lead a sex retreat for a bunch of middle schoolers.

Had I not been so horrified, it would have been comical. I'd only been married a month. Who was I to lead such a retreat?

Turns out, I needn't have worried.

The sex retreat curriculum was abstinence-only.

At the time, that didn't bother me. I was young, conservative, and had grown up being taught abstinence-only. I assumed that since that's all I'd ever heard from the church, that's what the church taught. Period. End of story.

In fact, I believed so strongly in an abstinence-only approach to sex that I even went toe-to-toe with my boss over one of the adult leaders she'd assigned to me. He was a divorced male currently living with his longtime girlfriend.

This infuriated my delicate sensibilities so much that I marched into my boss's office and told her—with all the conviction a twenty-one-year-old know-it-all has—that under no circumstances would I lead a sex retreat with this man. How could I when he was clearly not following God's plan for sex?

Fast forward six years, when I took high schoolers on a retreat where they wanted to talk about sex. I pulled out the same abstinence-only curriculum I'd used on my first retreat, modified it for a high school audience, and facilitated it. For the first time, I included an anonymous survey that asked teens about their sexual behavior.

Their answers horrified me.

My church kids weren't so innocent after all.

Now, I'd heard statistics suggesting that "nearly two thirds of teenagers have intercourse at least once before college,"[1] yet I'd convinced myself that the teens in *my* youth ministry were different since they were church kids.

I should have known better.

As I read through my teens' surveys, I realized that while they desperately needed to talk about sex in a safe space, the conversation I'd prepared wasn't going to cut it. An abstinence-only retreat didn't match the lived reality of my teens, nor did it meet them where they were in terms of their theology. They saw no disconnect between being sexually active and following Jesus.

I was left with two choices. I could either force my teens to conform to a theology that I was no longer sure was scripturally accurate, relevant, or God-honoring, *or* I could reevaluate that theology in hopes of finding a more effective way to minister to teens.

Curiosity combined with my teens' needs drove me to reevaluate my sexual theology. Through extensive study, I concluded that faithful Christians have—for centuries—interpreted what Scripture says about sex differently. While many faithful Christians advocate an abstinence-only approach to sex, others advocate a more whole-person approach to sexual ethics. Knowing this opened the door for me to begin reimagining what a faithful conversation with teens about sex might look like.

MY ASSUMPTIONS AND THEOLOGICAL ANCHORS

As I've searched through Scripture in my quest to better understand what it says about sex, I routinely return to four ideas that now serve as my theological anchors in my conversations with teens about sex.

Because God created our bodies, they and sex are good

The first theological premise that anchors my conversations with teens about sex is the imago Dei. This theology affirms that "God created human beings in his own image…male and female he created them."[2]

Because we are created in God's image, our bodies are good. They reflect God. And because they do, "…the man and his wife were both naked but they felt no shame."[3]

Did you catch that?

There is nothing shameful about our bodies—even our genitals.

To put it another way, our bodies are not evil. As author Bromleigh McCleneghan says in her book, *Good Christian Sex,*

> Our bodies *are* us. We are human creatures, which means we are body and soul, made in the image of God, made with bodies. The

key profession of our faith is that God was not against taking on a body, and so did! God came to live among us in Jesus Christ (Philippians 2:6-8, among others).[4]

Unfortunately, Christians tend to forget this. Instead, we make the goodness of our bodies conditional on things like how modestly we dress, and we make the goodness of sex conditional on being married.

The problem is that when we make God's good gifts conditional, we make them about us (and what we do or don't do) rather than about the One who created us. When our focus turns inward, sex becomes as broken as we are. It becomes about our own self-gratification, which makes it easy to objectify our partners, and even to intentionally (or unintentionally) degrade, humiliate, and exert power over another person.

That is NOT God's intent for sex.

According to Genesis 1:31 (NLT), "God looked over all he had made and he saw that it was very good."

All that God made includes us. It includes our bodies—and sex.

We are—each and every part of us—*very good*, because that's how God made us.

Sex is what defines biblical marriage

Within Christendom and, in particular, evangelicalism, there's a powerful subculture called purity culture. It teaches young people to abstain from sex until marriage, where marriage is defined "biblically" as one male and one female.

The problem is, it's hard to create that definition of marriage from the pages of Scripture.

In Scripture, marriage includes polygamy (case in point: Jacob's marriage to Rachel *and* Leah in Genesis 29:14-30) and the taking of wives who "please you" from your enemies (Deuteronomy 21:10-14). Biblical marriage also condones paying for your bride (remember the time King David bought his wife Michal with the "lives of 100 Philistines" in 2 Samuel 3:13-14?) and the practice of arranged marriage (Isaac and Rebekah in Genesis 24).

The most consistent aspect of biblical marriage is actually sex. According to Scripture, when two people have sex, they're "united into one" and therefore married (Matthew 19:4-5). As Jesus says in Matthew 19:6 (NLT), "Since they are no longer two but one, let no one split apart what God has joined together."

According to Scripture, sex is what marries someone—not something you suddenly get to do once you're married to someone. As conservative author Mo Isom writes in her book, *Sex, Jesus, and the Conversations the Church Forgot,* "Sexual acts always tie souls… Sex is one of the most powerful agents of unification, devotion, and surrender."[5]

Scripture's highest aim isn't your virginity

The goal of purity culture is to preserve someone's virginity until marriage. As a result, purity culture adherents often ask teenagers to demonstrate their commitment to purity by signing an abstinence-only pledge, which are often made in high-pressure environments that play on teens' emotions.

Because abstinence-only pledges typically define virginity as the state of never having had penile to vaginal intercourse, an "anything but" culture often results that implicitly encourages teens to do "anything but" have intercourse. This explains why "male [True Love Waits] pledgers are four times more likely to have anal sex than other young people, and pledgers of both sexes are six times more likely to engage in oral sex."[6]

Here's the thing, though. Although Christians like to obsess over their virginity, Scripture doesn't.

One passage illustrating that Scripture's highest aim isn't our virginity is 1 Corinthians 6:12-13 (NLT), which says,

> You say, "I am allowed to do anything—but not everything is good for you. And even though "I am allowed to do anything," I must not become a slave to anything. You say, "Food was made for the stomach, and the stomach for food." (This is true, though someday God will do away with both of them.) But you can't say that our bodies were made for sexual immorality. They were made for the Lord, and the Lord cares about our bodies.

When it comes to sex, the question teens ask more than any other is, "How far is too far?" Teens want to know what they can and cannot do. Christian teens want to know how far they can go without sinning.

According to 1 Corinthians 6:12-13, though, Scripture's focal point is not how far is too far. It's not whether or not you're still a virgin. It's whether or not something is actually good for you. Instead of asking, "How far is too far?" Scripture raises the question, "Is sex good for me in *this* time and place with *this* person?" While the first question emphasizes an arbitrary boundary, the second emphasizes relationships—between people and God. As a result, it gives teens a very different framework for making sexual decisions.

Another key passage in conversations with teens about sex is 1 Thessalonians 4:3-8 (NLT), which says,

> God's will is for you to be holy, so stay away from all sexual sin. Then each of you will control his own body and live in holiness and honor—not in lustful passion like the pagans who do not know God and his ways. Never harm or cheat a fellow believer in this matter by violating his wife, for the Lord avenges all such sins, as we have solemnly warned you before. God has called us to live holy lives, not impure lives. Therefore, anyone who refuses to live by these rules is not disobeying human teaching but is rejecting God, who gives his Holy Spirit to you.

According to this passage, Scripture's aim isn't our virginity, it's our holiness.

God's design for sex is that we control our bodies. No matter how much we might like to, we cannot control someone else's body. A female cannot control a male's lustfulness by wearing modest clothing. Likewise, as youth workers, we cannot control our teenagers' bodies. We cannot set someone else's sexual boundaries for them. What we can do is engage in honest conversations with teens about what it means to control their bodies so that they can live with holiness and honor.

A key part of helping teens understand what it means to control their own bodies and live in holiness and honor is consent. To give consent means to give permission for something. Consent is a critical component of sexual education and responsibility that's often overlooked in religious conversations.

Controlling our own bodies means that no matter how much we might desire someone or something, we will not act on that desire unless our partner consents to it. Since consent is about controlling our bodies *and* honoring others, it involves ongoing conversation. Consent always needs to be explicit; it should never be implicit. It can, however, be withdrawn at any point. If a teenager participates in oral sex once, it doesn't mean they've consented to it indefinitely.

Consent is also an important part of a healthy marriage. Being married to someone doesn't give one person the right to do whatever they want to the other person's body, whenever they want. That's abuse. It's the opposite of what it means to control your body and honor that of your partner.

Scripture enables us to form a God-honoring sexual ethic
If Scripture's highest aim isn't to keep people virgins until marriage, what is it?

It's to equip us to love and honor God. It's to empower us to follow Jesus.

When it comes to sex, the way we do that is by forming a Scripture-based sexual ethic—a set of moral principles used to determine what's healthy and right.

One Scripture passage that's useful in formulating a sexual ethic is Micah 6:8 (NLT), which says, "…O people, the Lord has told you what is good, and this is what he requires of you: to do what is right, to love mercy, and to walk humbly with your God."

While churches commonly engage young people in conversations about social justice, few engage them in conversations about sexual justice. In a culture in which an increasing number of people are recognizing the prominence of sexual crimes and exploitation—including by public officials—this must change.

One way to change that culture is to apply Micah 6:8 to our sexuality by asking questions like:

- When it comes to our sexual expressions, what does it mean to do what is right? How does doing what's right enable us to love God, ourselves, and our neighbor?

- Within the context of a sexual relationship, how can we show mercy?

- Within the context of a sexual relationship, how can we—together with our partner—walk humbly with God?

Asking—and more importantly, answering—these questions helps teens understand that sex isn't just about *their* pleasure, it's about serving someone else.

Another key passage in establishing a healthy sexual ethic is Matthew 22:37-39 (NLT), in which Jesus says,

> "'You must love the Lord your God with all your heart, all your soul, and all your mind.' This is the first and greatest commandment. A second is equally important: 'Love your neighbor as yourself.'"

Once again, you can apply this passage to sexuality by asking teens questions like:

- How can we use our bodies—including our sexuality—to love God with all our heart, mind, and soul?
- How can we establish a sexual ethic that focuses on others and enables us to love, honor, and respect ourselves, our partners, and God?

When we help teens apply passages like Micah 6:8 and Matthew 22:37-39 to their sexualities, we equip them to follow Jesus in every aspect of their lives. We are giving them the critical thinking skills needed to establish a sexual ethic that serves them well throughout their entire lives and enables them to love God and others.

That's discipleship.

MY PRIORITIES

When discussing sex with teens, I have several priorities I want to communicate with them, all of which stem from my theological anchors.

God is FOR us

It might seem strange that in a conversation with teens about sex, the first thing I want to communicate is that God is for them. Yet, whenever I talk with teens about sex, I'm reminded how much teens believe the church—and therefore God—is anti-sex, rather than sex-positive. According to the Barna Group, one reason why young Christians leave the church is that their church experiences related to sexuality are often simplistic and judgmental.[7]

Because many teens associate the church with abstinence-only teaching, they think that God doesn't want them to have any fun. Others look at this teaching as antiquated since "the age of first marriage is now commonly delayed to the late twenties."[8]

In reality, however, God is unequivocally *for* us, an idea that comes from Romans 8:31 (NLT), which asks, "If God is for us, who can ever be against us?"

For God to be *for* us means that God loves us. God accepts us for who we are, which, not coincidentally, is also how God made us.

Because God is for us, God wants what's best for us. Both the law and the gospel reflect God's best for us.

Because God is for us, our bodies and sex are good. There is no place for shame in conversations about sex. We need not feel ashamed of our bodies, nor do we need to feel ashamed of anything we have (or haven't) done sexually. After all, as Paul writes, "nothing can ever separate us from God's love"—not even the loss of our virginity.[9]

Teens don't have to be afraid to discuss sex with adults
Often, fear dominates conversations with teens about sex.

We fear that when we talk with teens about sex, they'll learn things about our pasts we'd rather they not. We fear they'll misunderstand us or, worse, lose respect for us. In reality, when we share vulnerably with teens—especially about our mistakes—teens tend to respect us more, not less.

Conversations with teens about sex also tend to be riddled with fear because we worry we'll only get one shot at them. In reality, though, these conversations are best had over the course of months and years, not days and weeks.

We also fear that teens will walk away from our conversations afraid of or dreading sex, or perhaps worse still, believing that anything goes.

And those are just our fears. Teens are equally afraid to talk about sex with us because experience has shown them that we'll talk *at* them, not with them. Teens fear we'll reject them if we learn they're no longer virgins. They fear that when it comes to sex, what they're feeling (and doing) isn't normal. Or worse, they fear they'll die virgins; that no one will ever see, know, and want to have sex with them; or that they're missing out on something that all their other friends are enjoying.

While these fears are real and we need to acknowledge them as such, nothing good happens when conversations about sex are rooted in fear. Fear makes us say and do dumb things. It makes us lash out at people in anger or withdraw into ourselves. Maybe that's why 1 John 4:18 (NLT) reminds us that "Love has no fear, because perfect love expels all fear. If we are afraid, it is for fear of punishment, and this shows that we have not fully experienced his perfect love."

That's why, as with all conversations with teens, discussions about sex need to be bathed in the love of Jesus, not rooted in fear.

It's more important to establish a sexual ethic than it is to establish sexual boundaries

One of the functions of adolescence is for teens to establish autonomy and independence, which means separating and distinguishing themselves from those they're closest to, especially their families. Often, this looks like rebellion, as teens vehemently disagree with what the adults in their lives are telling them. In actuality, it's often teens exercising their newly discovered critical thinking muscles to decide for themselves what they believe and why.

Given this, we do teens a tremendous disservice when we attempt to tell them what to do (e.g., give them sexual boundaries they need to follow) without helping them to understand why they're important. That's why it's important to talk *with* teens about sex, not *at* them.

It's also why it's important to help teens wrestle with how their desire to follow Jesus impacts every facet of their lives, including their sexual decisions. The best way to do this is to intentionally help teens formulate a sexual ethic.

Sexual ethics help us to "order our lives and relationships, while being flexible enough to respond to a variety of unforeseen situations."[10] They are value-centered, where values are defined as "The deepest-set of rules that guide one's decisions."[11] According to author and sex educator Al Vernacchio, "Values don't just tell us what we do; they tell us why we do it, which is much more important. Our values reflect our core beliefs; they tell us what really matters to us."[12] They "help you determine what's right in an ethical, moral, or spiritual sense."[13]

Because values reflect a person's core beliefs, the values of Christians reflect a Christian worldview, including the reality of sin, where sin might be defined as

> [the] force within us and in our communities and world that pulls us to do, as Paul puts it so beautifully in Romans, "the evil I do not want"... Sin hurts people and thus it's important to name it, stop it, and work for healing and justice.[14]

Values don't arbitrarily name sexual boundaries. Instead, they give people a lens through which they can decide (among other things) what their sexual boundaries are. To put it another way, sexual ethics give people a filter through which they can determine how best to love God, themselves, and their neighbors.

While the sexual boundaries that teens set for themselves often change as they age, a well-formed sexual ethic rooted in their values will remain constant and equip them to continually make God-honoring decisions about a host of important facets of their lives, including sex.

Consider a high school student who might commit to abstaining from sexual intercourse as a freshman but wonder as a college senior how she can continue to realistically honor her commitment to purity, especially if she's still unmarried at the age of thirty. In contrast, if that high school freshman is instead taught how to form her own sexual ethic, that might well carry her through into adulthood.

For example, a sexual ethic that says, "sex binds me deeply to another person" might cause a high school teenager to decide he doesn't want to be bound to someone in that deep a way and, as a result, to abstain from any sexual behavior that results in an orgasm. But as that person moves into adulthood and matures (in every way), that same sexual ethic might lead him to conclude that it's okay to engage in various sexual behaviors with a person he wants to be bound to (as long as there's mutual consent and satisfaction and honor of the other person, both inside and outside of the bedroom).

Additionally, the development of a whole-person sexual ethic removes the focus from remaining a virgin and, instead, encourages teens to think critically about how they can do justice as well as love God, themselves, and others through their sexuality.

MY PLAN

As someone who started her career in youth ministry by unashamedly embracing a conservative, abstinence-only sexual education approach, my perception was that those with more progressive stances taught teens that "anything goes." In fact, that's something I've heard my conservative peers echo time and time again. What I've since realized is that progressive doesn't mean permissive; it doesn't mean anything goes. With that in mind, here are the specific strategies I use to help teens formulate a sexual ethic of their own that's whole-person centered, sex-positive, and still rooted in Scripture.

Recognize the unique role the church has in talking to teens about sex

Most schools teach sex ed in their curriculum at some point. They typically cover the basics—names and functions of male and female genitalia as well as how things (including condoms) work. In sex ed classes, one person (the teacher) typically presents the information while everyone else consumes it. The church can take a very different approach to sex ed by making it discussion-oriented. Discussions allow you to teach by intentionally guiding the conversation. That gives teens the chance to participate in difficult conversations that help them decide for themselves what they believe and why. When teens do that, they're far more likely to adhere to the values and sexual ethics they set for themselves long-term.

Typically, schools cover sex education during a particular grade. However, because teens are constantly changing—physically, emotionally, and spiritually, not to mention in terms of their maturity—you can't just talk about sex once and assume you've addressed everything you need to. For that reason, in my ministry, we typically talk about sex once in middle school and twice in high school (every other year). We talk about sex once in high school through a four-week series during our regular youth gatherings. The other time, we hold a "sex retreat," where we go away for a weekend (Friday through Sunday) and discuss sex, typically through five sessions rich in content.

Because churches are different than schools, we intentionally cover different material than schools do during sex ed. Since most sex ed classes cover the basic plumbing (so to speak), we don't have to. Instead, we can just cover enough of the basics to give everyone a common language for discussing them. One of my favorite ways to do this with high schoolers is to post sheets of paper around the room labeled with a sexual organ, like *penis, vagina, vulva,* and *breasts.* I then ask teens to walk around the room and write down any words they've heard used to describe the body part listed. Afterward, I have an adult leader read each list aloud before guiding teens in reflecting on why we call sex organs by so many words other than their rightful names.

As part of this, we talk about what, if anything, people notice regarding the difference in names given to male and female sex organs and what that suggests about our culture's perception of gender and sex. Then, we decide what we'll call various sex organs during the remainder of our series. Doing so dignifies teens and models the maturity I expect from them during our conversations. It also gives them language to use when discussing sex with their parents and future partners.

Because many teens have had sex ed elsewhere, they come into church with preconceived understandings of what sex is. However, not everyone's definition is the same. For this reason, before you get too far into your conversation about sex, you need to actually define it. When you say *sex* are your teens thinking about intercourse, or are they thinking about something else?

Many teens have been taught that sex is penile-vaginal intercourse. While some readily accept that definition, it makes others uncomfortable, especially those who are LGBTQ or who have friends who are. Teens often find that in order to come up with a definition of sex that works for both straight and gay people alike, their definition of sex must be broad enough to include things like oral sex or the achievement of an orgasm. However, that makes a lot of teens uncomfortable because of its implications on their virginity. If oral sex is *actually* sex, then many teens in our youth ministries are no longer virgins.

That's why it's so important to help teens realize that Scripture's highest aim is our holiness, not our virginity. This is another key aspect of what distinguishes conversations about sex in youth ministries from the sex ed classes that teens participate in at school.

That's also why it's so important to incorporate Scripture each time you have a discussion on sex. Explore what Scripture says about our bodies, sex, sexuality, desire, temptation, singleness, marriage, justice, and what it means to love God, ourselves, and others. A great place to start is by using the passages outlined in the assumptions and theological anchors section of this chapter. As you explore those passages, don't randomly pull out isolated verses. Instead, look at Scripture in context. Explore those passages that affirm your perspective as well as those you find difficult to explain. Instead of looking at Scripture only to find answers to the "How far is too far?" question, wrestle with how Scripture guides us in our quest to more fully love God, ourselves, and others in all aspects of life, including our sex lives.

Encourage questions

As you explore what Scripture says about our bodies and sex, questions will naturally arise. When they do, encourage teens to ask them.

One great way to do this is to invite teens to submit their questions via text or a question box. If you use a question box, take time early in your series to ask everyone to write down a question at once. This enables those who truly have questions to ask them without drawing attention to themselves. When the expectation is that everyone has questions, it's less awkward for any one person to ask one. Assure teens that they can submit their questions anonymously and that you won't spend hours analyzing their handwriting, attempting to figure out who asked what.

During my ministry's last sex series, the sex question box was a huge hit. Teens asked questions including:

- Is period sex okay?

- Was Jesus really a virgin?

- Do people have sex in public places?

- How do I tell someone "no"?

- How do I talk to my parents about sex?

- Is premarital sex a sin?

- If sex is so beautiful, then why didn't Jesus have it?

Regardless of what questions you receive, dignify them by taking them seriously and wrestling with them together. Involve your adult leaders in this process by directing specific questions at them and allowing them to answer based on their sexual ethic and understanding of Scripture, rather than along one unified party line. When teens hear a variety of Christian perspectives on what it means to follow Jesus in all aspects of their lives, it shows them the diversity that exists both within the Christian tradition and within your congregation. That, in turn, helps them envision how they might develop and live out their own sexual ethic.

Help teens articulate and define their values

There are several reasons for engaging Scripture with teens as you discuss sex. Scripture grounds teens in the story of their faith, which shapes who they are as people. Scripture also shapes our values, which, in turn, dictate what rules we adhere to. If a rule aligns with our values, we willingly, though not always easily, follow it. Understanding our values, therefore, helps us understand why we believe what we do. Values ground our actions.

For this reason, getting practical with teens in conversations with them about sex means addressing values. It even means identifying what values we bring to Scripture and what values we gain from Scripture. One way to do this is to openly discuss values as we read Scripture passages related to sexual themes.

For example, youth workers often explore the story of David and Bathsheba during the course of a series on sex in order to talk about temptation. I've done so as well. I used to read the story a few verses at a time, occasionally stopping to ask, "Is this a sin?" My goal in doing so was to help teens decide when in the story David moved from temptation to sexual sin and therefore answer the question, "How far is too far?"

Over the years, however, I've learned that in addition to this being the wrong question, this approach robs teens of the opportunity to think critically about their sexual behavior and how they can use it to love God, themselves, and others. What's more, focusing on boundaries actually robs people of their dignity. It places a higher value on following a rule than on loving and respecting the other person in a relationship. When that happens, it's all too easy to objectify someone and to trample over that person's desires, to think that as long as you're doing what's allowed, nothing else matters (including whether or not your partner has actually consented to what you're doing).

A better approach to this same story is to read it through a values lens. As in the previous example, walk through this story verse by verse, occasionally stopping to assess whether or not David's actions are wrong. However, don't stop there. Go deeper. Ask teens to identify what value(s) led to their conclusions. Doing so challenges teens to think critically about not just their actions, but the values that govern them. This helps them understand why they actually believe something is right or wrong. That, in turn, leads to convictions. And convictions prepare teens to identify their own core values and articulate a sexual ethic that flows from them.

Another way to help teens identify their values is to compile a list of the values that govern their families, their friends, and the organizations they're a part of, including their schools and church(es). Then challenge teens to wrestle with whether or not they actually agree with those values. Ask them whether those values are theirs or someone else's. According to Al Vernacchio, values are actually a teenager's when they are:

- "Chosen freely from alternatives after careful consideration of its consequences. It cannot be something thrust upon us or adopted without significant forethought."

- "Prized and publicly affirmed when appropriate. If we're ashamed of it, won't talk about it, or won't defend it to others when called upon to do so, it isn't a value."

- "Acted on consistently and repeatedly. If we say it but don't do it, it's not a value. If we follow it sometimes but not consistently, it's not a value."[15]

Once teens have wrestled with which values are actually theirs, ask them to make a values board (either in a journal or in some creative way) that reflects *their* top five values: the statements and ideas that govern how they live, love, and interact with the world around them. Because it can be difficult for people to articulate their values, it can be helpful to give teens a formula for their values statements. One I've used that works well is

I value _____

because _____.

The values of teens vary greatly. Teens' values might include things like:

- I value grades because they're the key to my future success.
- I value my family because I know that they love me unconditionally.
- I value friends because they help me understand who I am.
- I value my job because I need to save money so that I can go to college.
- I value my teammates because without them, I know I can't succeed.

Once teens have constructed their values statements, give them the chance to share their values with others (usually in a small group environment, which promotes greater safety) and process their experiences together using questions like:

- How easy or difficult was it for you to choose your five core values? Why do you think this is?
- Look at your core values. How many of your core values relate directly to your body, your gender, sex, or sexuality? Why do you think this is?
- Even if your values don't relate directly to your sexuality, what might your values suggest about how you treat others you're in a relationship with?
- Based on your values, what is and isn't acceptable sexual behavior for you to engage in?

Teach teens to use their values to formulate and articulate their sexual ethic

Once teens have articulated their values, it's time to move into a more explicit discussion about boundaries and sexual ethics. Remember, a sexual ethic is a set of moral principles used to help someone determine what is and is not healthy and good. It involves boundaries but is not limited by them. Instead, it's more whole-person focused. While boundaries might change with life stage, a well-defined sexual ethic can remain constant throughout someone's life—regardless of whether they're young or old, single, coupled, or married.

To help teens formulate and articulate their sexual ethic, summarize (or have your teens summarize) the key components of your conversation thus far. This essentially generates a list of your group's theological underpinnings and priorities. Doing so also gives you a chance to reexamine key Scripture passages and ideas.

Generating that list is the communal part of this practice. Once you've identified your group's theological underpinnings and priorities, give teens time to formulate and articulate their own sexual ethic. It may or may not resemble yours. That's okay. The goal in helping teens form a sexual ethic is to help them develop *their* sexual ethic, not yours.

One of the best ways to help teens articulate their sexual ethic is to invite them to write a letter to themselves, which you'll mail back to them two years later. Because articulating their sexual ethic can feel like a daunting task for teens, it can be helpful to give them prompts to consider as they write. Some of the prompts that I've used for this include:

- How is God *for* you?
- Do you really believe that God created your body and sex to be very good? Why or why not?
- What does it mean to love God—even through your sexuality?
- What's required to love yourself—including the body God gave you?

- How can you love others through your sexual behavior?

- When is sex "just" and "unjust"?

- What values and principles will you use to determine what, if any, sexual behaviors are healthy and good for you at any given point in time? What scriptural support can you find for those values and principles?

- How will your values, principles, and understanding of Scripture impact your sexual decisions?

- How, if at all, might your sexual boundaries change as you get older?

- Could your boundaries change without violating your sexual ethic? If not, what would you have to change about your sexual ethic for it to be applicable not just now, but ten years from now? How could you make those changes in a way that doesn't violate your interpretation of Scripture?

Teens can choose to answer some or none of these prompts as they articulate their sexual ethic. They're simply there to help frame this activity.

After giving teens ample time to write their letters, collect them (in sealed, self-addressed envelopes so that they know that no one—including you—will read them). Finally, process the experience with them.

It's been incredible to see how God has used this practice in the lives of my students. When teens receive these letters, I regularly hear how they arrived at "just the right time." Because the letters are values based rather than boundaries based, they typically don't elicit shame. Rather, they serve as tangible reminders that God is *for* them—in every aspect of their lives, including their sex lives.

Model what it means to be faithful in adhering to your sexual ethic
As teens work to develop their sexual ethic, it's important for them to hear the sexual ethics of others, as well as their impact on people's

lives. This is a great place to utilize adult leaders. Unlike when I first began my career in youth ministry, when it comes to talking with teens about sex I'm now thankful for adult leaders who offer different perspectives than mine. I want to serve alongside people who are LGBTQ, males and females, single, dating, married, and divorced. And I want teens to hear from each of these people about how they faithfully follow Jesus in their lives, especially as it pertains to sex.

Set up your adult leaders for success by coaching them on what is and isn't appropriate to share with teens. Since details are typically what get people into trouble, encourage leaders to share openly and vulnerably, but without the specifics they'd give to their peers. When in doubt, ask adults to ask themselves this question: For whose benefit do I want to share this information? If it's for the benefit of the teen listeners, it's typically okay to share; if it's to get something off their chest, it's not. Additionally, remind adult leaders to tie their sexual ethic to Scripture.

One of my favorite ways to engage adult leaders is to interview them about their sexual ethics. Interview single adult leaders. Ask them about their dating lives, including how they decide who to date. Invite them to share about how their faith impacts their decisions about dating, sex, and how to follow God in and through their relationships with others. Let them talk openly about the beauty and messiness of being single. Give them space to share some of their sexual ethics with students as well as how that impacts their sexual decisions.

In the same way, interview married adult leaders about what married life is like. Ask them how they do justice in their marriages and how they love God through their relationships with their spouses. Let them share about the challenges of marriage, as well as the joys. Give space for them to share some of their sexual ethics with students as well as how that impacts their sexual decisions.

When I interviewed my adult leaders during our most recent sex retreat, they shared from a variety of vantage points. One had been married for decades. Others were single with very different sexual ethics. One dated regularly and often, very casually. Another believed wholeheartedly that as a follower of Jesus, you should only date someone if you could see yourself marrying that person. Her sexual ethic said that sex should be reserved for marriage; another adult leader believed it should be reserved for committed relationships; still another thought that as long as consent and respect were present, sex could be a part of most relationships between two adults.

All adults shared their honest perspectives—as well as how faith had contributed to them. In this way, teens learned not just from married couples but from single adults struggling to follow Christ and live out their sexuality in a way that honored God. The result was far more complex and, in some ways, messier than it would have been had we ensured that every adult leader on our teaching team was married or sexually pure. And yet it was also far more beautiful. It gave teens a glimpse of the diversity within the body of Christ and a variety of different role models, each living out what it means to faithfully follow God in this important aspect of life.

Repent and ask for forgiveness, collectively and individually

Forgiveness is a key part of any conversation about faith, and certainly of one about sex.

As a college student, I remember being taught to ask for forgiveness for those times I went further than I should.

Doing that certainly isn't wrong, but it might be missing the point.

There are things in our sexual lives that I wholeheartedly believe we need to confess and repent of. But those things aren't primarily (or mostly) boundary violations. They're ways in which we fail to love God, ourselves, and others. They're ways in which we fail to respect others and treat them with the inherent dignity that all humans have because we're created in the image of a God who loves us and is for us.

One of the best ways to address repentance and forgiveness with teens is to explore the story of Judah and Tamar in Genesis 38. This story gives you an opportune way to wrestle with values, sexism, patriarchy, rape, sexual misconduct, forgiveness, and redemption. After grappling with these topics in the context of the story, discuss the ways in which our culture—and sometimes our churches— intentionally or unintentionally condone sexism, patriarchy, rape, and sexual misconduct today.

Once you've done that, read and discuss Psalm 51, which David wrote after his royal screw-up with Bathsheba. Explore the ways in which David repents—or turns away—from his sinful behavior.

Then invite teens to either individually or collectively do the same by writing their own Psalm, naming and repenting of the ways they've either sinned or condoned behavior that is unjust or that fails to show love to God and each other. When teens are willing, invite them to share their Psalms with one another, in small or large groups as well as at your youth ministry's worship.

Involve parents

As with so much of faith formation, the impact of your conversation with teens about sex increases if you involve parents. Prior to your sex series, e-mail parents an outline of the series along with questions they can use to prompt discussion with their teens afterward. Also consider holding a parent meeting prior to your sex series. Share content with parents. Facilitate discussions designed to equip parents to have conversations with their own teens about sex. Additionally, ask parents to write their teens letters that you'll give the teenagers during a specific week of your sex series (or, if you're covering the material at a retreat, during a specific session).

If you invite parents to write a letter, give them a specific prompt (this will make it easier for most parents to actually do this). In the past, I've asked parents to write letters in response to the following prompts:

- To you, what does it mean to have a healthy sexuality? Why?
- How did or has your faith informed your sexual behavior? Why?

- Imagine that when it comes to healthy relationships, you are your teen's role model—in friendships, dating, and marriage. What do and don't you want your teen to emulate from your life? Why?

- How would you describe your sexual ethic? Who or what helped form it?

These prompts are deep. They invite parents to be vulnerable with their teens and, hopefully, to share stories their teens have not yet heard. They also require parents to spend time writing their letters (and they require you as a youth worker to spend time following up with parents to ensure that every teen receives a letter).

If you involve parents via letters during your series on sex, set up the experience well for the teens in your ministry. Integrate the prompt you gave parents into what you're talking about with your group. Explain to teens that you invited their parents to speak to them through letters. Then invite them to spread out around your space and read their letters. Pay attention to their emotions. Affirm that whatever they're feeling is okay. Once teens have finished reading their letters, process the experience together using the following prompts:

- In one word or phrase, describe your reaction to receiving your letter from your parents.

- What, if anything, surprised you about the contents of the letter from your parents?

- What did you learn about your parents from their letter?

- What, if anything, do you better understand about your parents after reading their letter?

- After reading this letter from your parents, what can you do to continue this conversation with your parents? What might you gain by doing so?

Incorporating parental letters into our series on sex has been one of the best things I've done in youth ministry. It gives parents a way to actively participate in an important discussion without encroaching on their teen's space. It also allows parents to talk about sex with their teens in new ways. Our prompts aren't typically what they address in the "birds and the bees" conversation many have already had with their teens. Parental letters also enable teens to get to know their parents differently. Parents often share things in a letter that they'd never share in person, which teens greatly appreciate. As teens come to see their parents differently, they often become more willing to engage them in ongoing, deeper conversations about sex.

FINAL THOUGHTS

At the first church I served, the day before I launched our annual sex series, a parent walked into my office, threw a condom on my desk, and said, "If you're talking about sex, you better be showing my daughter how to use this."

I was horrified. I couldn't believe this mother expected me—a Bible-believing youth pastor—to give her daughter a condom.

Sixteen years later, I still don't do a condom demonstration in our annual conversation with teens about sex. However, I'm no longer horrified by this concept—even (or perhaps especially) as a Bible-believing youth pastor.

Instead, I've come to understand that the Bible is simultaneously less and more clear than I once thought it was about sex. It's less clear on acceptable boundaries because its ultimate goal isn't our virginity, it's our holiness. It's our ability to follow Jesus and love God, ourselves, and others. That's what the Bible is clear about.

That clarity has much relevance to how we talk with teens about sex.

Not long ago, I ran into a former student, Brooklyn. She informed me that our youth ministry's sex retreat was the most important thing we ever did (or discussed). When I asked why, Brooklyn responded by saying, "Because you didn't just tell us what we could or couldn't do. You made us think about it and set our own boundaries."

Upon hearing this, I asked Brooklyn, "Did you keep them?"
She responded with an enthusiastic "Yes!"

It says something when a twenty-eight-year-old single female points back to your ministry's sex retreat as the most pivotal thing she did in your ministry.

Our approach worked because we didn't obsess over boundaries. Instead, we gave Brooklyn the tools she needed to think critically about her faith, interpret Scripture, formulate her own sexual ethic, and then apply that sexual ethic to her life. In the process, Brooklyn discovered that her sexuality wasn't removed from her faith; it was an integral part of it. She realized that God wasn't a curmudgeon trying to prevent her from having fun, but rather someone who is unequivocally *for* her.

That shaped Brooklyn's life—not just in high school, but as a college student, and as a young adult seeking to follow Jesus by loving God, herself, and others.

When our approach to talking with teens is about more than behavior modification and getting them NOT to have sex, all kinds of wonderful things happen, perhaps the most important of which is that teens leave our ministries with an integrated, consequential faith that matters to their daily lives.

RESPONSE

JONATHAN MCKEE

When I was a teenager, I was the master at finding loopholes in rules. When I heard my first sex talk, which happened to be heavy on boundaries and light on explanations of "why," I immediately sought out the loopholes.

If only I'd felt safe enough to talk with someone about my sexual activity, maybe I could have made better decisions.

That's where I love Jen's heart. Jen obviously longs to create a safe space to talk with teenagers about sex. So many teens don't have this and end up looking for answers on their own, usually in the wrong places.

I share Jen's frustration with incomplete teaching. I'm annoyed with someone who would teach that only intercourse is off limits outside of marriage. I'm even more irritated with anyone who would teach that sex is "naughty." (Has that person even read the Bible?) These teachings are not only unbiblical, but they show a lack of understanding of the teen mind. The teen mind always asks why, and never settles for "because I said so."

I love Jen's desire for a "whole person" approach to sexual ethics. She obviously doesn't merely want to teach a bunch of boundaries, but help teens explore biblical holiness. More people should explain sex in the context of the entire biblical story.

We see how Jen's passion developed where she writes about her first experiences talking with youth about sex. She was handed a curriculum apparently very "boundary" heavy, and lacking in expressing the big picture. So in her effort to understand her teens' needs better, she conducted a survey. The results of this survey opened Jen's eyes to a couple of sobering truths:

1. These teens were far more sexually active than she predicted

2. The boundary-heavy curriculum seemed irrelevant to these teens, and didn't provide real world answers for them, at least, not the ones they were looking for

Here's where Jen took a leap to a place I never would have landed. Her bad experiences with the "abstinence-only" approach led her to believe that we shouldn't teach biblical boundaries at all, only the desire for holiness.

Now, I'm excited that Jen claims Scripture's aim is to equip us to love and honor God and empower us to follow Jesus. But there are definitely ways to provide a "whole person" approach to sexual ethics without abandoning the loving boundaries God created for us.

Jen wants to teach a holistic approach, avoiding shame-based tactics or any notion that virginity is the ultimate goal, but her fear of teaching boundaries leads her to make some pretty grandiose claims, like, "According to Scripture, sex is what defines biblical marriage," and to convey that there is no such thing as biblical marriage. Jen desperately needs to reexamine some of the very passages she quotes, like Genesis 1 and 2, which clearly lay out God's design for marriage—"That is why a man leaves his father and mother and is united to his wife, and they become one flesh." (I guess I'm missing how that sounds like sex marries someone?) The Ten Commandments, Jesus, and Paul all support this idea of biblical marriage. We shouldn't let Old Testament narratives about imperfect people like Abraham, Jonah, and King Solomon confuse us. Sexual immorality or adultery are never okay, even if Judah did it. The fact is that Jesus tells us not to commit adultery. In fact, he tells us not to even think about it (Matthew 5:28).

Jen writes, "It's more important to establish a sexual ethic than it is to establish sexual boundaries." It would be better if she said, "It's critical to establish a sexual ethic that goes beyond merely setting sexual boundaries."

Jen also writes, "focusing on boundaries actually robs people of their dignity. It places a higher value on following a rule than on loving and respecting the other person in a relationship." Again, it's obvious that Jen doesn't want us to *just* teach boundaries. But that doesn't mean there are none. Jesus says several times, "If you love me, keep my commands" (John 14:15). That doesn't mean don't ask questions or sit down and write out your own ethics (scary). It means that Scripture is where these ethics come from. And the more we get to know Jesus, and allow his Holy Spirit into our lives, the more these loving boundaries will make sense. Obeying his commands is an expression of our love for him. This is probably why he says, "Those who accept my commandments and obey them are the ones who love me…" (John 14:21a, NLT).

Jen, I echo your desire to get teens into Scripture passages like Micah 6:8 and ask them powerful questions about Matthew 22 (questions like, "How can we use our bodies, including sex, to love God with all our heart, mind and soul?" This is a great question!). But please don't abandon his commandments just because of someone else's bad teaching about them.

Let's truly do what you said: "the way we honor God is by forming a Scripture-based sexual ethic."

VIEW 4: EMBRACING GOD'S DESIGN FOR US AND FOR SEX

JOEL STEPANEK

I went to my first youth conference as a freshman in high school. I encountered Christ in a powerful way, gave my life to him, and resolved to live as a disciple. It was at that same conference that I learned the Catholic Church's teaching on sexual ethics—well, at least part of it. It happened in a session where the men and women split off from each other and a speaker told us the dangers of pornography, masturbation, and premarital sex. He explained that we were called to chastity and that, by living into this virtue, we would be honorable men. It sounded great to me, and after a clip from *Braveheart* and a call to action, I was sold. They passed out chastity commitment cards. I signed mine and put it in my wallet.

It was 2001.

In the following months, the Catholic Church shuddered under revelations of the sexual abuse of minors. To this day it continues to wrestle with the dynamics of hierarchy and power that can create a breeding ground for sexual abuse. The apparent hypocrisy within the Catholic Church coupled with an emphasis on sexual ethics within mainstream culture presents no small challenge for those seeking to teach teenagers about God's plan for sexuality and help them adopt from it a consistent sexual ethic and morality. For teens, all of this is further complicated as they navigate the many additional challenges they are faced with as they date and explore intimacy.

This isn't the first moment in history when people have wrestled with or misunderstood the Catholic Church's teaching on sexuality. On July 25, 1968, Pope Paul VI wrote a landmark document for the Catholic faithful called Humanae Vitae, which focused on the regulation of birth, or, colloquially, birth control. As more Christian denominations at the time were becoming accepting of birth control, including the use of hormonal contraceptive methods, there were increasing calls for the Catholic Church to reevaluate its stance on the use of contraception, which forbid all contraceptive methods other than natural family planning. In fact, several individuals consulting with the pope proposed allowing condom use within marriages. It seemed, in the midst of the sexual revolution taking place in America at the time, that the Catholic Church would change its historic stance on birth control.

Humanae Vitae, though, did not reverse this teaching, but instead affirmed it in no uncertain terms. The document was historic because it caused a divide among Catholics, especially in the United States. It signaled to many of them that the bishops guiding the Catholic Church, and the pope himself, were disconnected from the lived experience of men and women who were married and wrestling with how to regulate or space their children. Not only that, but the notion of a celibate hierarchy (since priests and bishops do not marry) speaking into matters of sexual intimacy seemed, to many, ridiculous.

All of that is important to understand because it highlights a key point: the Catholic Church's stance on sexuality needs to be taught in such a way that it can be understood within the current cultural context, something that didn't occur with Humanae Vitae. This is especially critical when it comes to teenagers. It's worth spending the time and effort to teach Catholic sexual ethics well, because there is value—for both Catholics and non-Catholics—in wrestling with the sexual morals of the Catholic Church. Looking back, it's easier to see the wisdom in Humanae Vitae. There were four things that Pope Paul VI wrote would happen if contraceptive use became widespread:

- Infidelity would increase and morality (on a whole) would decline
- There would be a loss of respect for women as they became objectified (which we've seen evidence of through the testimonies and stories that have surfaced through the #MeToo movement)
- Power would be abused
- People would begin to believe that they had "unlimited dominion" over their own bodies

It isn't difficult to argue that in many ways these predictions have become reality.

There is wisdom in the Church's teaching on sexuality and sexual ethics. Regardless of our exact faith traditions, both Catholics and non-Catholics can recognize these realities and that alone should warrant at least a further inspection of what Catholic tradition can offer teenagers in the realm of sexual morality.

Though challenges exist—the Church's teachings on contraception, same-sex attraction, gender and identity, and the purpose of sex stand in contradiction of our current Western cultural understanding—that doesn't make the Church's teaching on sexual morality any less true or any less liberating for Christians, particularly teenagers. The fullness of the Catholic Church's sexual teachings needs to be presented well and whole to young people. They may be challenging teachings, but they are logical ones.

Which brings me back to that youth conference I attended in 2001. Although the speaker gave some good points, they weren't grounded in anything other than "good boy/bad boy" theology. I looked at my body, my desires, and my sexuality all as very bad things. After all, those were the things that led me to sin. The words I heard at that conference didn't help. Nor did they give me an understanding of actual sexual ethics from a Catholic perspective. A few days after the conference I ripped the chastity card to pieces.

MY ASSUMPTIONS AND THEOLOGICAL ANCHORS

After the widespread confusion and, in some cases, outright rejection of Humanae Vitae, in the late '70s through the mid-'80s Pope John Paul II (now a canonized saint in the Catholic Church) wrote and delivered a series of talks specifically revealing God's plan for sexuality. These talks (called "audiences") provided a much-needed framework for understanding the Catholic view of human sexuality. They were given specifically to help people understand Humanae Vitae.

This series of talks actually totaled 129 audiences—that's one long sermon series. There were several additional talks that were never presented, but all were later compiled into a work called *Man and Woman He Created Them: A Theology of the Body*.[1] For most Catholics, this document is simply referred to as *Theology of the Body*.

The teachings are not anything new, but are likely the best synthesis of Catholic sexual teaching that exists to date. Before diving into how we can present this teaching to teenagers, understanding the basic theological underpinnings is critical. What follows is an outline of the material found in *Theology of the Body* that should be understandable for any Christian teenager, especially of this current generation (iGen or Generation Z). People of any faith tradition can dialogue with the Catholic understanding of sexuality and employ some of the methods I suggest to teach sexuality to teenagers.

Catholic sexual morality, as outlined below, certainly falls on the more conservative side, but diverges from more stringent sexual ethics in some surprising ways.

First, within Catholic theology one is not "doomed" to sin, nor are we totally depraved. We rely on God's grace. Once that grace is received at our baptism, and continually received through the sacraments, prayer, and communion with God, we must draw upon it for any good act, and in order to have faith.

That said, it is not necessary that we sin. Of course, we do sin and maybe even sin often. But a key theological difference from other schools of thought (and one that is beyond the scope of this chapter) is that we are not bound to sin. The tendency toward sexual sin is not a death sentence.

Second, we are composite creatures with both bodies and souls. Since our bodies and souls are linked, what we do with our souls impacts our bodies and what we do with our bodies impacts our souls. This means that there are times when we must work to heal physical afflictions in order to heal spiritual ones. This is particularly important when it comes time to speak about addictions.

Third, our sexuality is good and a gift from God, but it can be distorted, meaning not used for its intended purposes. The intended purposes of the act of sex are procreation and unity.

Fourth, there are two sexes and they correspond with gender—biological sex and gender are intrinsically linked and cannot be separated. This is part of God's design. That said, it does not mean that people who experience a disconnect between their biological sex and their gender identity are sinful or evil, nor should we discriminate against them.

Fifth, sex is reserved for a man and woman who are married. It is only within a marriage covenant between a man and a woman that sex can be unifying and procreative. Sex within marriage between a man and a woman is free, total, fruitful, and faithful (more on this follows later in the chapter). Expressions of sex outside of marriage and/or occurring in ways that are not free, total, fruitful, and faithful are distortions of God's intention, and are not good.

Finally, our sexual identity is an important *part* of our identity, but is not our entire identity, and sex is not the greatest good we can experience. It is possible to forgo sexual relationships and live in meaningful, impactful, and loving relationships with others.

Those are the basics. I feel guilty even writing them out this way because each is deserving of many more words of further explanation, but I hope that over the coming pages I'll be able to do that as we explore how to impart this critical knowledge to teenagers.

MY PRIORITIES

"What do you want?" In the Gospel of John, this is the first question Jesus asks. It seems to be a question that Jesus is fond of—he asks all kinds of variants of it. The gospel writers were all intentional about the "first impression" Jesus gets in their work. It is no small matter that John wanted the first words we read from Jesus to be "What do you want?" (John 1:38).

We all want something—we seek and we desire—but teenagers are seeking in a special and important way. The psychologist Erik Erikson said that the critical developmental task of adolescence is identity formation.[2] Teenagers are trying to find out who they are. Compounding this search is a desire to be known, but also a fear of being known and judged or rejected. Modern technology gives teens new platforms to explore their purpose, allowing teenagers to document their inner lives (or what they claim to be their inner lives) on social media, where those inner lives will be consumed, assessed, praised, or criticized by others.

Though the mediums change, the desire to be known does not. It is fundamental, and as teenagers begin to date they look for someone to fulfill that desire. They are seeking something—but perhaps more specifically, they are seeking someone.

For many young people, this desire isn't merely something developmental, but more like a longing or even an ache. They may even describe their longing to be known by another person as painful. Part of that longing comes from a desire for intimacy and, thanks to puberty, a developing sexuality. Young people quickly learn that when their desire to be known meets their sexual desire, the act of sex seemingly fulfills both. And they aren't wrong. They were designed that way.

But they may also feel something else when both of those desires are expressed, whether through sexual intimacy with another person, or through experimentation with pornography and masturbation alone: a sense of being empty and ashamed. If those same teens attend a youth group any time prior to or after their sexual experiences, they may hear teaching about sexual ethics that seems to compound these feelings of shame. They learn that these kinds of sexual expressions are a sin. They may hear that what they are doing isn't part of God's plan and that they need to wait for marriage.

But for many of them, marriage is ten to fifteen years away. How can this seemingly great thing be so off limits and cause such shame?

It doesn't seem fair. Why would they have these desires and impulses if acting upon them is wrong?

Why did God create us this way?

Our desire for love, connection, and intimacy is rooted in something big, and teens need to know that. That's why the first key to talking to teens about sex is:

Identify their desire for love and help them understand where it comes from

Too often we jump right into the details of sex, sin, and God's plan. It isn't surprising; when a church or school brings in a "chastity speaker" or a Christian speaker to talk about sex and marriage, they often just want that person to give a list of dos and don'ts so that teens will understand what boundaries they shouldn't cross. The problem with these lists of rules without heart or real context is that people will inevitably break those rules (see: the Ten Commandments). If teens don't first understand that God gave us our desires—even our sexual desires—and that those desires point us toward a reality bigger than the immediate moment, no "sexual sin" talk is going to work. We desire God. The desire for God is written on the human heart (Catechism of the Catholic Church 27). God made us, and God made all that is within us. He designed it all for a purpose and a plan. Our longing for union with another reveals our deeper longing for union with God. Saint Augustine famously wrote in his *Confessions*, "O Lord, our hearts are restless until they rest in you." Our desires—all of them—point us back to God.

Our desire for food points us back toward our desire for the daily bread, the bread that satisfies, that only God can provide.

Our desire for love and intimacy points us back to the love that never fails us and the God who is love.

Our desire for sex points us toward a desire to be wholly given to another as a gift and to receive another totally as a gift.

We can't get rid of our desires, but some people do try to suppress them. If not properly understood and ordered, though, our desires are maddening. If our desire for food is disordered, we develop an eating disorder. If our desire for love is disordered, we will do anything we can to feel loved, even if we know it isn't healthy.

If our desire for sex is disordered, we seek pleasure but are never satisfied.

Any desire can become disordered when we try to suppress it or use it incorrectly. If we seek to suppress our sexual desires because we believe they are evil and sinful, we miss the beauty of what our sexuality was created for. If we use our sexuality outside of the intended purposes, we abuse the gift.

Christopher West, a popular Christian author and authority on John Paul II's *Theology of the Body*, identifies three attitudes when it comes to our desires, and makes them analogous to how we might approach food. We can either starve, settle for fast food, or wait for the banquet.[3]

These three categories are especially helpful for teens in starting to understand how they are approaching their desires. By helping them identify that they are wrestling with the ache of desire, they will know how to approach Christ, who ultimately satisfies our desires, through prayer.

When it comes to understanding desire, the first approach to go over with teens is starvation. When we address our desires through a lens of "starvation," we see all desire as disordered or evil. In turn, we seek a deprivation of desire and likely experience a lot of shame. The goal of starving our desires is to rid ourselves of them completely. A person reasons that if he or she can get rid of desire, he or she will be free from sin and actually find joy. An analogy certainly could be made to Buddhism, which teaches that the freedom from suffering comes in ridding ourselves of desire (since desire leads to suffering).

From a Christian perspective, this view is problematic. First, we are body and soul beings. Yes, we need to keep our desires in check and not let them rule us, but to deprive ourselves runs contrary to our human nature. Our basic desires for food, water, shelter, and love are not bad—but our experience of them may be bad. When it comes to sexual desire, there are a number of things that may push a teen toward a starvation view.

It is possible that they come from a household that views sex, the body, or sexuality as dirty, shameful things. A puritanical view of sex and sexuality can easily lead to a sense of shame or guilt at even common sexual feelings. For example, let's think about how we respond when a thought comes into our heads or when we see a suggestive image. We can't control when this happens, but we can control what we do after the thought or image comes into our minds—we can choose not to dwell on it. For someone who sees the world through a starvation lens, though, simply having the initial thought (as unintentional as it may have been) is unacceptable.

The major issue with a starvation lens is that it is not sustainable. Author Rob Bell writes in his book *Sex God* that we can't look at ourselves as angels because we have bodily needs.[4] When we ignore or attempt to suppress those bodily needs and desires, it can backfire, and the pendulum can swing the other way.

Bell also notes in his book that while we can't be angels, we aren't animals, either. We are more than our bodily desires.

For many people, distorted desires are not related to starvation, but to eating the wrong thing. If a person is viewing his or her desire through the lens of a "fast food diet," that person is simply consuming anything he or she wants, regardless of the negative impact. Many people live with this mentality. The indulgence of their sexual desires reveals a lack of understanding of what real union is for.

For many people, this isn't because they are actively rejecting God's plan for sexuality; they simply don't understand what sex actually means and the purpose for which it was given to us. Many teenagers have been poorly educated or miseducated about their sexuality. As a result, they seek to appease their desires in ways that ultimately aren't satisfying.

Think about it—if you never knew what good, healthy food was but were told your whole life that fast food was good for you, you would attribute every aspect of your poor health to something other than the food you were eating. After all, you've been told that the fast food is not a problem. Yet you can't escape the effects of the poor diet.

Now imagine if, one day, someone revealed to you what healthy eating was and how it could change your life. You might be skeptical at first. You might even be angry. This person is insulting everything you've ever known. Yet, a part of you might feel like this person is right. After all, you've been feeling terrible and don't know why, and now there might be an explanation.

For many teenagers, this is the reaction they will have when they hear about God's plan for sex and sexuality. When they realize their desires can point them to something bigger, a change begins in their hearts.

The "banquet lens" is the final lens Christopher West suggests, and it is where we want to move teenagers. We want them to view their desires in terms of a banquet. Our desires are good things and point us toward something even better, but they also need to be directed. If we starve ourselves and decide that all food is bad, then we won't want to eat the banquet. We will miss out on the good. If we are binging on fast food, on the other hand, we won't be ready for the infinitely better things that are prepared for us. When the banquet is offered, we might not even want it. But if we can be disciplined, we can experience something better.

We must embrace our desires and order them toward something bigger. This is the second key point in talking to teens about sex:

If teens don't get the gospel and understand that they are meant for heaven, they will never understand sexual morality

This is an area where the Catholic Church has room to grow. We make assumptions that people know the gospel because they come to Mass, but this isn't necessarily the case. In fact, I would wager that— though I have heard the gospel proclaimed at Catholic youth groups, conferences, and retreats—there are many Catholic teens who haven't heard the gospel yet. If we assume the people we're teaching know the gospel, we often miss something key.

Catholic sexual morality involves a tension. We believe sex is good and a gift from God, but it isn't a gift everyone gets all of the time, even in marriage. As a result, there is that ache and longing where our desires need to be reordered. But what do we order our desires toward? We order them toward heaven. Our desires only make sense in light of heaven, because that is where all desire is fulfilled. If teens don't get that, it is really hard to tell them to wait to have sex or to stop other behaviors that are not leading to holiness.

When we order our desires toward heaven, though, they can be transformed. We can only receive the grace we need to order our desires this way by accepting the gospel message and seeking to follow Christ.

And why do we need the gospel, and why do we need to reorder our desires? Because our desires can easily become distorted. This, again, is true of any desire, not just sexual desires. A person who develops an eating disorder experiences a disordered desire for food (either in wanting to avoid food or to overeat). A person with a disordered desire for love may accept treatment that is less than what he or she deserves. This is the third talking point for teens:

Our desires are distorted because of sin: while at their root our desires are good, the way we act upon them may not be good

This talking point focuses on sin and our need for a savior. It isn't hard to talk to teens about this need, because they see these distortions of desire in the world all of the time. Whether it is human sex trafficking or the objectification of the human body, they see people treated without the dignity they deserve. They may experience shame at consensual sexual experiences that they realize were not fulfilling, or they may know somebody who is a victim of sexual assault, where the desire for sex was acted out in a violent manner. Teenagers are exposed to pornography at alarming rates. They know how broken our sexual desires can be.

We as youth workers have to help teens make the connection between the brokenness our world experiences in the realm of sexuality and how the Christian faith can offer more.

Going from recognizing the distortions we commonly experience in relationships to teaching about sexual morality isn't actually a stretch—Jesus taught about it. Distortions in relationships existed in the time of Christ. In the Gospel of Matthew, Jesus is challenged to give a teaching on divorce, a practice Moses permitted. The Pharisees ask Jesus a sort of trick question. Nonetheless, Jesus takes the hard question and turns it on its head.

> And Pharisees came up to him and tested him by asking, "Is it lawful to divorce one's wife for any cause?" He answered, "Have you not read that he who made them from the beginning made them male and female, and said, 'For this reason a man shall leave his father and mother and be joined to his wife, and the two shall become one flesh'? So they are no longer two but one flesh."
> (Matthew 19:3-6, RSV)

Divorce is a distortion, and Jesus calls it out. Divorce wasn't in God's plan for marriage. In confronting the distortion of what marriage was meant to be, Jesus appeals to "the beginning," and pulls references from both Genesis 1 and 2. This passage is key, especially for our modern teaching on biblical sexual morality. Many people will boldly proclaim that "Jesus never taught about sex," but this passage provides us with a clear example of Jesus providing the theological foundation for sexual ethics. It also emphasizes the importance of the beginning chapters of Genesis in understanding sexuality. These early chapters establish the existence of a male and a female gender and biological sex that reflect God, the complementarity of these two sexes, and the union that the two share, which is expressed in marriage and allows them to be "one flesh."

That relationship between Adam and Eve, though, was distorted. And from that moment forward, the man would seek to dominate the woman and the woman would seek to dominate the man. Lust entered the picture as the two would try to use one another. The effects of distorted relationships play out today. The passage continues,

> They said to him, "Why then did Moses command one to give a certificate of divorce, and to put her away?" He said to them, "For your hardness of heart Moses allowed you to divorce your wives, but from the beginning it was not so."
> (Matthew 19:7-8, RSV)

Jesus uses this example to explain why Moses allowed divorce— people have hard hearts. But, through Jesus, hard hearts are converted.

111

This isn't to say that there aren't legitimate reasons for divorce or separation—there certainly are. We can attribute those reasons to the unfortunate sickness of sin in our lives. When talking to teens about sex, though, we need to be able to appeal to these first chapters of Genesis and the way that God intended things to be, and recognize that divorce and separation are not what God wanted for marriage. That's why they are such tragedies when they occur.

The biggest distortion that exists between men and women as a result of the fall is the distortion that turns our desire to give ourselves as a gift to one another into a desire to use each other. After the fall and original sin, we no longer see each other as people made in the image and likeness of God, but rather as objects to be used. This doesn't usually happen out of malice; we simply want someone to fill our ache and longing for love. But, if we aren't able to give ourselves to the other person in return, we will wind up just using him or her.

We have to be able to start here, then, when it comes to talking to teens about sex. We need to ask the same question Jesus is asking, "What do you seek?" When a teenager is having sex, looking at pornography, or engaged in other sexual behaviors, we need to step back and ask them, "What do you want, really?"

The answers might be varied, but many will reply that they want to feel a connection, to express love, to feel desired, to feel pleasure or "feel good," or to not feel lonely. Some may be using sexual behaviors as an escape or a coping mechanism for something else.

In essence, any of these responses can be summed up the same way: we want to feel known and loved.

The next point when talking to teens about sex is this:

We are seeking union with God, and until we acknowledge and accept that, we will not be able to have healthy relationships

These words can be tough for teens to hear, but they are still necessary (and not just for teens, but for all of us). If we aren't allowing ourselves to be loved by God and to love God, we are always going to seek something else to fill that spot—but nothing else can fulfill it. Our desire for love and intimacy can be fully realized only in a relationship with our creator. If we expect creation to fulfill that desire, we will always be left short.

At the very worst, this leads us to use people (sometimes lovingly and sometimes not) in order to feel better about ourselves. That isn't how God designed our relationships to be.

When we live in a relationship with God, we experience what a healthy relationship actually looks like. We experience what it means to receive someone as a gift because God, in his mercy, extends his very life to us as a gift. We receive God and we, in turn, offer ourselves back to God. This happens in a pure way on the part of Jesus Christ through his cross and resurrection. That free gift from Jesus is our model of what it means to love another. When we love someone, we are willing to suffer for that person.

We all, ultimately, need to be purified through that same cross. The cross shows us the highest form of love: loving someone enough to even die for them. It also shows us that beyond that death, there is new life.

MY PLAN

Talking to teens about sex, especially from a Catholic perspective, requires an understanding of the framework laid out above: working through our desire, sin, and the ways that the cross helps correct our distorted desires. Really, though, this framework is necessary for the Christian perspective. Without an acknowledgement of the ache and desire we all feel for intimacy and love, we can't begin to talk about the expression of sex. Once we get that groundwork laid, though, the rest comes simply:

Recognize that sex is not the greatest good; self-sacrifice is

It is easy to glamorize and glorify sex to the point of idolatry. That talk I went to in 2001 did. The speaker (and many like him) meant well. He wanted to "redeem sex" by letting us know it was good—in the right context. The problem was that he told a room of 1,500 high school boys that sex was awesome, and we all needed to wait to experience that. He made it seem like sex was the ultimate good, rather than one good thing.

Western culture already promotes sex as the greatest good. In movies, in shows, in music, and in advertising, the message is clear: "Sex is the best thing there is—so have as much of it as you can with anyone you can, so long as it is safe and consensual."

Sex is absolutely a good thing, because we know that our bodies (and therefore our sexuality) were made by God. However, we cannot let our teaching convey sex as the greatest good. It simply isn't true. There are two additional reasons: first, in making it out to be the greatest good we simply frustrate teenagers. Second, by making it out to be the greatest good we isolate teenagers who experience attraction to the same sex.

This point cannot be understated: without understanding that sex is not the greatest good, we cannot reach teenagers. Sex certainly is important. When God allows humanity to be fruitful and multiply, he is allowing us to participate with a principle quality of God: God creates. Sex, for that reason, is incredibly powerful because it allows us to also create. God makes a man and woman in Genesis and gives them souls, but then he allows those two people to make more people (whom God also gives souls).

Is sex powerful? Yes. Necessary? Absolutely. But is it the greatest good? No—because love is the greatest good. Specifically, *self-sacrificial* love is the greatest good. When we are able to give ourselves in love to others—that is, be self-sacrificial for the good of another person—we participate in the greatest good. When two spouses have sex, they experience an aspect of the greatest good. But, that same couple may also express self-sacrificial love in a variety of other ways.

Similarly, an unmarried man or woman may also experience the greatest good in acts of service and in deep and abiding friendships.

We can say that, when a married couple has sex that is open to life and unifying, they experience self-gift—in other words, self-sacrificial love—and therefore the greatest good. However, that is only insofar as sex is in the proper context and the greatest good is not limited to sex.

The proper context for sex is when it can be expressed in a way that is faithful, fruitful, total, and free. These four aspects can only be fulfilled in a marriage between a man and a woman. So, that is the next talking point for teens:

Explain that sex is good, but is only good when it is faithful, fruitful, total, and free

We can pull three of these four qualities from Genesis (and subsequently Matthew 19), and the last we pull from a biblical understanding of love.

First, sex is faithful. Biologically, sex bonds two people together. Again, this is part of God's design. Teens need to be reminded often of the biological and spiritual crossover that is present in sexual ethics. Fidelity in a relationship puts sex in a proper context.

Second, sex is fruitful. It is open to life. This is a key component of Catholic sexual teaching. The act of sex must be ordered toward procreation. This was the sticking point in Humanae Vitae. Contraception is contrary to the purpose of sex because it interrupts the natural order for which sex was intended. At the most basic biological level sex does two things: it creates new life (or is at least open to the potential of it) and it also bonds couples within certain species of animals. Humans are one of those species. To remove the potential for fruitfulness (or to no longer allow sex to be ordered toward procreation) is to diminish what sex was designed to be. This means that sex, as an act, is only within the proper context when it occurs between a man and a woman.

Third, sex is total. When Jesus references how God created male and female to become "one flesh," he is referring to totality. Those of us entering marriage do so desiring to hold nothing back. Of course, because of our sin, we may struggle to give ourselves "totally" to another person. But in marriage, we try to give of ourselves to our partner completely. This includes not keeping secrets or hiding aspects of our lives from our spouse. If we do so, we are not being fully honest with our spouse, and we risk distorting what sex and our bond were created to be.

Finally, the very nature of love means that it must be freely given. Without free consent, sex is always disordered.

After talking with teens about sex and pointing out that it's designed to be faithful, fruitful, total, and free, there are a few more key things to emphasize.

Remind teens of God's love and mercy

One of the worst analogies to use when talking with teenagers about sex is, unfortunately, a youth ministry "classic." A speaker says to imagine seeing your bride or groom on your wedding day, but then also seeing all the people he or she has previously had sex with. This is a visual meant for people who have never had sex, designed to discourage them from losing their virginity prior to marriage. Among several issues with this is that it immediately shames people who have already lost their virginity. After all, there is "no going back" on what has been done, and now they are going to be lugging those past relationships with them to the altar someday. It also may cause some teens to think, "Well, since I've already screwed up, what is the point of trying now?" Other young people may simply look at themselves as "damaged" and believe that because of their choices, God could never accept them.

This is absolutely contrary to the gospel. Jesus Christ makes all things new. When talking with teens about sex, emphasizing God's mercy is key. Sadly, there are fewer and fewer teens whose lives have not been impacted by sexual sin. What they need is mercy, not condemnation.

We have to proclaim God's plan for sex because it is liberating—but we also need to remember that mercy heals.

Emphasize that victims of sexual violence are not guilty

In any group of teens it is likely that there are several who have been victims of sexual violence. They may feel like they have somehow sinned and are at fault for what happened. Talking about sex provides an opportunity for those teens to share their experiences with trusted adults and begin to find healing, but not because they've sinned.

Be aware when you are talking to teens about sex that there are people with these experiences who may not even realize they were the victims of violence, and others who are very aware of the hurt that was inflicted upon them. Never assign blame to a victim, but always offer the hope of God's healing and love, and then provide resources for counseling and fulfill any mandatory reporting requirements.

Be aware that some teens identify as LGBTQ and are feeling isolated, discriminated against, or angry

There are likely teens in your group who experience same-sex attraction, or identify with a gender other than their biological sex. Conversations about sex, especially in the Catholic tradition, present pastoral challenges. For many of these teens, the teaching seems unfair and discriminatory. It appears antiquated and behind the times—in many Western cultures, marriage to someone of the same sex is legal and celebrated. Sadly, there are also many parts of the world where individuals in same-sex relationships are persecuted and even killed.

It is important to emphasize that the Catholic Church actively teaches against unjust discrimination against individuals who identify as LGBTQ. The United States Conference of Catholic Bishops has released numerous statements regarding the pastoral care of individuals who experience same-sex attraction, and the Catechism of the Catholic Church notes that the genesis of same-sex attraction is unknown. This means that, when talking to teens about sex from this perspective, it is important to refrain from offering reasons why a person might be experiencing same-sex attraction. It also means that there is not necessarily a "cure" for teens who identify as gay or lesbian. Some people experience same-sex attraction as a transitory experience that changes after their adolescence, but others experience it for a lifetime. Regardless, all people are called to order their sexual desires in a way that recognizes God's plan for sexuality. For some this means marriage and for others it means directing the desire for love and intimacy into service, friendships, and companionship with others.

Provide practical ways to love and serve now

When we invite people out of a certain set of behaviors and into new ones, there is a tension because a void is created where the old was. For teenagers this is especially crucial to recognize. Once we've recognized that sex is not the greatest good, it becomes easier to provide some practical advice for loving others and experiencing friendship and intimacy in ways that don't involve sexual activity.

These practical ways of loving and connecting with others may look different for every teen and community but, regardless of the context, they need to be a focus of the conversation. The best context for giving any practical advice is the cross and the concept of self-gift. How can teenagers give of themselves to others? Through service, engaging in friendships, participating actively in their families? Since we are made to love sacrificially, practicing sacrificial giving helps teenagers experience fulfillment.

When we talk with teens about love, we also need to note that love involves both suffering and joy. This is key, and will help teens identify relationships where they are using others or being used.

Suffering, in this context, does not mean that teens should allow somebody to hurt them. Rather, it means caring about someone in a way that when the other person hurts, we hurt too. It is the kind of suffering we feel when we experience compassion for another person (the word "compassion" literally meaning "to suffer with"). When we really love someone, we feel what that person feels. For many people, this definition of love is scary. We want the joy that comes with love, but not necessarily the vulnerability that leads us to the potential for suffering or hurt.

Our joy in our relationships comes in proportion to how willing we are to suffer alongside those we care for. Practicing compassion in friendships not only boosts the quality of those relationships, but also will help teenagers find true and healthy fulfillment of their desire to be in relationship with others.

Ultimately, if we want to know love, we need to practice compassion. In doing so, we find joy.

The final key to talking with teenagers about sex is to walk with them

These are big topics that lead to big questions and big conversations. After Jesus asked, "What do you seek?" he didn't just leave things open-ended. He called the disciples to follow him. He journeyed with them. They had conversations. He didn't abandon them or give them a quick teaching. He walked with them. There is a lot for us to take away from that as we talk with young people about sex. The reality is that these conversations with teens aren't one-time occurrences that happen at a single youth group gathering we host once each year. They are conversations that involve big questions, the gospel message, sin and the fall, our desires and goodness, and who God calls us to be. They revolve around our identity and our call to love and to give of ourselves to other people.

When I walked out of that youth conference in 2001, I did rip up that chastity card only a few days later. But I kept all the pieces. I put them in my wallet and carried them around, a sign that I wasn't perfect but striving. I am grateful for the many people who walked with me and helped me to grow in my understanding of who God was calling me to be. For many teens, the journey is like that. It won't involve one commitment but many recommitments, as well as the efforts of dedicated individuals who seek to help teens grow in their relationship with God. These are people who are willing to have the big conversations, provide the difficult answers, and offer mercy and compassion along the way, all the while recognizing that some big questions may not have clear-cut answers, or even seem to have answers at all right now. Being willing to walk alongside a young person in that tension is critical.

FINAL THOUGHTS

God created all things and created them good. In fact, after the addition of humanity, he calls the whole of creation "very good." Creation is ordered toward something greater than what we see. It mirrors a divine reality. Sex is a part of creation, as are our bodies. They are not dirty, flawed additions to God's perfect creation, but part of it. We struggle to see and embrace that because of sin.

But sin doesn't diminish how powerful sex is. It is the process by which we create life! Our desires for intimacy are designed to point us back to God. Sin does distort those things, though. Teenagers are no strangers to this distortion. If we address the symptoms of the distortion but not the root cause, we may win teenagers in the moment, but we will never capture their hearts. We need to look at the root of desire—where it comes from, and why—and help young people understand what they are really seeking through intimate connections with others. We need to help them identify the ways in which their current expressions of desire may be leaving them unfulfilled.

This is no small task. There are entire industries built upon the idea that we can fulfill our deepest longing for eternity with consumable goods. Still, by embracing the challenge and entering into the "ache" of teenagers as we talk about sex, our sexuality, and the root of our desire, we not only present the beauty of what sex is intended to be, but also a vision of who we are created to be—integrated, whole, and holy persons.

RESPONSE

JAKE KIRCHER

I am a denominational mutt, having had experiences in many different kinds of churches, yet one exception has been the Catholic expression of faith. Growing up in a more conservative Evangelical setting, I have heard numerous assertions, and frankly warnings, about the differences between the Catholic tradition and more Protestant traditions. With this in mind, it gave me joy and a sense of appreciation to read Joel's chapter and find so much that I can agree with and affirm.

Our own experiences as teenagers are almost identical regarding the "good boy/bad boy" theology of sexuality that we both received from our churches, and I can recognize the exact same drive in Joel that I have to make sure that, as youth workers, we create a healthier narrative for the teens we work with. I also much appreciate and respect the common understanding of healthy sexuality being centered around the gospel, the work of Christ, and the fact that we are all creations of God.

Our area of most agreement perhaps comes in the fact that "sex is not the greatest good we can experience." As stated in my own chapter, I believe that both our secular culture and faith culture have made sex an idol, putting far too much focus on our fulfillment and our sinful nature, respectively. Helping teens understand both that sex is not the entirety of their identity and that their sexual desires are a gift from God is crucial. In other words, sex and sexual desire are very good, but are not absolute goodness in our lives.

Two areas of this chapter left me with questions, in part due to my more limited understanding of Catholic theology. The first is regarding the starvation attitude as expressed by Christopher West. Joel wrote, "Yes, we need to keep our desires in check and not let them rule us, but to deprive ourselves runs contrary to our human nature." How can this be taught and affirmed while coinciding with the Catholic teaching of celibacy for its leaders? Could this lead to a dimension of teaching that centers around "Do as I tell you, not as I do," and if so, how useful is that message for the teens hearing it?

My second question is centered around the Catholic teaching that sex must be "fruitful" and "open to life." As someone who went through infertility treatments for years, I know firsthand the disappointment and feelings of failure when you can't get pregnant as a couple. Because of this, I wonder how this view is taught in a way that doesn't lead to more guilt and shame for teens who later in life may have similar experiences. Further, after adopting and a miracle pregnancy that was very difficult, to suggest that sex is now diminished for my wife and me because we then surgically prevented "the potential for fruitfulness" is difficult to comprehend. Why do the creation of life and the neurological bonding through sex have to go hand in hand for it to be considered good?

My most significant disagreement with Joel comes in his final priority: "We are seeking union with God, and until we acknowledge and accept that, we will not be able to have healthy relationships." My first concern with this is based on the fact that practical experience has suggested that this isn't true. I know many non-Christians who would acknowledge the opposite—that they aren't seeking union with God, yet have fantastic, healthy relationships. Likewise, after working in churches for fifteen-plus years, I know *many* people who are (or at least say they are) seeking God, but who have horrible relationships. To me, this priority gets too close to a proposed formula that could set teens up for disappointment in God and faith because it doesn't always work.

My second concern with this is that in the Genesis 2 creation narrative, Adam is with God in the garden midway through creation and there is no other person there to fulfill him. God is the one who points out that this isn't a good thing (see Genesis 2:18). Part of being created in God's image means that we are wired to need others and be fulfilled through our relationships. In fact, it is other people, specifically those who are different from us, who help us grow, mature, and become more like Jesus. The greatest commandments go hand in hand: love God and love others. We must hold those in a paradoxical tension and not in a hierarchy; otherwise we could find ourselves in unhealthy, Pharisee-like relationships.

NOTES

Fostering Open, Positive Dialogue | Jake Kircher

1. Newell, J. Philip. *The Rebirthing of God: Christianity's Struggle for New Beginnings* (Woodstock, VT: Christian Journeys, 2015), 98.
2. To a certain degree, sex would look similar to what is depicted in Hulu's *The Handmaid's Tale*: a ritualistic act, devoid of any God-given humanity, solely for the sake of reproducing.
3. "The Ethics of F***ing (Part 1)." *The Liturgists*. Podcast audio, April 4, 2018.
4. McIlhaney, Joe S., and Freda McKissic Bush. *Hooked: New Science on How Casual Sex Is Affecting Our Children* (Chicago, IL: Northfield Publishing, 2008), 16.
5. McKnight, Scot. *The Blue Parakeet: Rethinking How You Read the Bible* (Grand Rapids, MI: Zondervan, 2008), 118.
6. Coontz, Stephanie. *Marriage, a History: How Love Conquered Marriage* (New York: Penguin Books, 2006), 106.
7. Ibid.
8. Johnson, Sue. *Love Sense: The Revolutionary New Science of Romantic Relationships* (New York: Little Brown & Co, 2013), 129.
9. Most of these were teens who had grown up in the church and came from solid Christian families, and some of their parents had been leaders within our church.
10. The police in the town where I worked for most of my direct youth ministry experience told me they started seeing sexual activity show up in sixth grade.
11. This series has been published as a downloadable curriculum by The Youth Cartel in *THINK Volume 4: Relationships & Sexuality* (San Diego, CA: The Youth Cartel, 2016).
12. For a much more detailed look at this philosophy of teaching, check out my book *Teaching Teenagers in a Post-Christian World* (San Diego, CA: The Youth Cartel, 2014). Or for a more specific look at how I have done this with the topic of sex, check out my curriculum *THINK Volume 4: Relationships & Sexuality* (San Diego, CA: The Youth Cartel, 2016).

Exposing Young People to Explicit Truth | Jonathan McKee

1. Martino, Steven C., Marc N. Elliott, Rosalie Corona, David E. Kanouse, Mark A. Schuster. "Beyond the 'Big Talk': The Roles of Breadth and Repetition in Parent-Adolescent Communication About Sexual Topics." *Pediatrics* Volume 121 Issue 3, 2008.
2. Anderson, Monica and Jingjing Jiang. "Teens, Social Media, and Technology 2018." PewInternet.org. http://www.pewinternet.org/2018/05/31/teens-social-media-technology-2018/.
3. Donovan, Jay. "The average age for a child getting their first smartphone is now 10.3 years." Techcrunch.com. https://techcrunch.com/2016/05/19/the-average-age-for-a-child-getting-their-first-smartphone-is-now-10-3-years/.
4. McKee, Jonathan. "3 Ingredients Catalyzing the Spike in Teen Depression." TheSource4Parents.com. https://thesource4parents.com/parenting-help/3-ingredients-catalyzing-the-spike-in-teen-depression/.
5. Szalavitz, Maia. "How Oxytocin Makes Men (Almost) Monogamous." Time.com. http://healthland.time.com/2013/11/27/how-oxytocin-makes-men-almost-monogamous/.
6. McKee, Jonathan. *Sex Matters* (Ada, MI: Bethany House Publishers, 2015).
7. Keller, Tim. *The Meaning of Marriage: Facing the Complexities of Marriage with the Wisdom of God* (New York: Penguin Books, 2013).
8. Fogelman, Dan. *Crazy Stupid Love.* Directed by Glenn Ficarra and John Requa. Warner Brothers, 2011.
9. Magary, Drew. "What the Duck?" GQ.com. https://www.gq.com/story/duck-dynasty-phil-robertson.
10. Centers for Disease Control and Prevention. "How You Can Prevent Sexually Transmitted Diseases." CDC.gov. https://www.cdc.gov/std/prevention/default.htm.
11. Centers for Disease Control and Prevention. "CDC Fact Sheets." CDC.gov. https://www.cdc.gov/std/healthcomm/fact_sheets.htm.

12. Centers for Disease Control and Prevention. "HPV and Men—Fact Sheet." CDC.gov. https://www.cdc.gov/std/hpv/stdfact-hpv-and-men.htm.

13. Centers for Disease Control and Prevention. "Chlamydia—CDC Fact Sheet." CDC.gov. https://www.cdc.gov/Std/chlamydia/STDFact-Chlamydia.htm.

14. National Cancer Institute. "HPV and Cancer." Cancer.gov. https://www.cancer.gov/about-cancer/causes-prevention/risk/infectious-agents/hpv-fact-sheet.

15. National Abortion Federation. "Abortion Facts." Prochoice.org. https://prochoice.org/education-and-advocacy/about-abortion/abortion-facts/.

16. For further reading, these are all questions I answer in detail in my book to teens, *Sex Matters*, referenced above.

17. The Global Children's Forum. "The Church Sticking Together—the Vital Role of Intergenerational Relationships in Fostering Sticky Faith." ChildrenEverywhere.com. https://childreneverywhere.com/stickyfaith/.

Developing a Sexual Ethic | Jen Bradbury

1. Orenstein, Peggy. *Girls and Sex: Navigating the Complicated New Landscape* (New York: Harper, 2016), 77.

2. Genesis 1:27 (NLT).

3. Genesis 2:25 (NLT).

4. McCleneghan, Bromleigh. *Good Christian Sex: Why Chastity Isn't the Only Option—And Other Things the Bible Says about Sex* (New York: HarperOne, 2016), 64.

5. Isom, Mo. *Sex, Jesus, and the Conversations the Church Forgot* (Grand Rapids, MI: Baker Books, 2018), 21.

6. Orenstein, Peggy. *Girls and Sex: Navigating the Complicated New Landscape* (New York: Harper, 2016), 89.

7. Barna Group. "Six Reasons Young Christians Leave the Church." Barna.com. https://www.barna.com/research/six-reasons-young-christians-leave-church/.

8. Ibid.

9. Romans 8:38-39 (NLT).

10. McCleneghan, Bromleigh. *Good Christian Sex: Why Chastity Isn't the Only Option—And Other Things the Bible Says about* Sex (New York: HarperOne, 2016), 71.

11. Vernacchio, Al. *For Goodness Sex: Changing the Way We Talk to Teens about Sexuality, Values, and Health* (New York: Harper Wave, 2014), 22.

12. Ibid.

13. Ibid.

14. McCleneghan, Bromleigh. *Good Christian Sex: Why Chastity Isn't the Only Option—And Other Things the Bible Says about Sex* (New York: HarperOne, 2016), 74.

15. Vernacchio, Al. *For Goodness Sex: Changing the Way We Talk to Teens about Sexuality, Values, and Health* (New York: Harper Wave, 2014), 25.

Embracing God's Design for Us and for Sex | Joel Stepanek

1. John Paul II. *Man and Woman He Created Them: A Theology of the Body* (Boston: Pauline Books and Media, 2006).

2. Erikson, Erik H. *Childhood and Society* (New York: W. W. Norton, 1950).

3. West, Christopher. *Fill These Hearts: God, Sex, and the Universal Longing* (New York: Image Publishing, 2013).

4. Bell, Rob. *Sex God: Exploring the Endless Connections Between Sexuality and Spirituality* (New York: HarperOne, 2012).

BIOS

Mark Oestreicher is a partner in The Youth
Cartel, which provides resources, training,
and coaching for church youth workers,
and is the author of many books for youth
workers, parents, and teenagers.
Twitter: @markosbeard.

Jen Bradbury serves as the minister of youth
and family at Atonement Lutheran Church in
Barrington, Illinois. A veteran youth worker,
Jen is the author of *The Jesus Gap: What
Teens Actually Believe about Jesus* (The Youth
Cartel), *The Real Jesus* (The Youth Cartel),
*Unleashing the Hidden Potential of Your
Student Leaders* (Abingdon), and *A Mission
That Matters* (Abingdon). Jen is also the

assistant director of *Arbor Research Group*, where she has led many
national studies. When not doing ministry or research, she and her
husband, Doug, and daughter, Hope, can be found traveling and
enjoying life together.

Jake Kircher has been working with teens,
families, and adults for fifteen-plus years as
a pastor, consultant, writer, and speaker. He
has been involved with local, regional, and
national organizations in various capacities
from speaking, communications, writing,
social media, and web design. A graduate
of Gordon College, Jake has been published

in *YouthWorker Journal*, *Group Magazine*, *Immerse Journal*, and
Relevant. He is the author of the THINK curriculum, has authored
the Viva curriculum for almost two years, and wrote *Teaching
Teenagers in a Post-Christian World*. Jake lives with his wife and two

kids just outside of New York City in Connecticut and is currently on staff at Trinity Church in Cos Cob, CT. You can find him on Facebook, Instagram, and Twitter as @jakekircher.

Jonathan McKee is the author of over twenty books, including *The Teen's Guide to Social Media & Mobile Devices* and *The Guy's Guide to God, Girls, and the Phone in Your Pocket*. He speaks to parents and leaders worldwide and offers free resources and training for youth workers at TheSource4YM.com.

For **Joel Stepanek**, what began as a simple internship in a parish youth ministry office evolved into an incredible adventure that's led him on numerous middle school lock-ins, high school retreats, parish missions, and ultimately to meet his wife, Colleen. Joel is the director of resource development for Life Teen International, where he creates engaging

youth ministry resources for middle and high school students. Joel is the author of *True North: A Roadmap for Discernment*, *The Greatest Job on Earth: The Seven Virtues of an Awesome Youth Minister*, and *Getting More Out of Confession*. He received his master's degree in religious education with an emphasis in youth and young adult ministry from Fordham University in New York City. Joel loves cooking, CrossFit, and spending time with his wife and two children, Elijah Daniel and Sophia Grace.

Made in the USA
San Bernardino, CA
10 January 2019